How to Look Younger & Feel Better to

Stay In The Game
Health, Beauty, & Fashion Tips for

Women Who Are 40+

by

Whitney Smith

Copyright 2015 by Whitney Smith

Published by Paxson Park Press

ISBN-13: 9780990704232

All rights reserved. Except for appropriate use in critical reviews or works of scholarship, the reproduction or use of this work in any form or by any electronic, mechanical, or other means now known or hereafter invented, including photocopying and recording, and in any information storage and retrieval system is forbidden with the written permission of the publisher

Smith, Whitney

Cover and Interior Design: Whitney Smith Cover Art by Katie Cadamatre
Eye Makeup Art by Lisa Daly

Paxson Park Press
700 Dean Court
West Chester, PA 19382

Table of Contents

Introduction

1. Understand Your Skin to Help Reverse the Signs of Aging — Page 11

2. 21 Habits of Women Who Look Younger Than They Actually Are! — Page 18

3. A Better Diet for a Younger, Healthier You, — Page 45

4. Vitamins & Supplements for Better Health — Page 62

5. Is Inflammation the Reason You Look so Old & Feel so Bad? — Page 84

6. Is Too Much Sugar Making You Look Older? — Page 97

7. Seven Most Outrageous Diet Myths — Page 102

8. Hair, Skin, Nails, and Makeup Tips — Page 112

9. Strike Beauty Gold with 10 All Natural Beauty Oils — Page 149

10. Are You a Fashion Victim?   **Page 157**

11. Gadgets and Gizmos   **Page 171**

**12. What If You Get Thrown Out
of the Game?**   **Page 178**

Selected Bibliography & Resources

Introduction
*"I am woman hear me roar
In numbers too big to ignore..."*

Helen Reddy

Back in 1972, when this song was first introduced and became a number 1 hit, feminism was coming into its own, and women were beginning to feel empowered. We were young, self-confident and ambitious, determined to establish ourselves as a force of nature.

Fast forward a number of decades, and now it does not seem quite so easy. Life has a way of knocking us down – and each time that happens it is harder to get back up. In truth, the deck is somewhat stacked against women. Society (and our parents) expect us to get married, then have children. That means interrupting our career path – even when we do return to work as soon as we can. If you take time off to get your kids into school, you really get off track, because technology in the workplace is moving at such a fast pace.

If you've had children, you know that another side effect is pregnancy weight which is very hard to lose. If you are juggling your role as mother and homemaker with a fulltime job, the stress can be overwhelming. Add to that, aging parents who need care, possibly a divorce and single parenthood, illnesses, widowhood – by the time we reach 40 or so, life has become quite challenging. And then...perimenopause and menopause strike!

The economy hasn't been very cooperative either. Downsizing, unemployment, foreclosure. It has been a nightmare for many of us. Because the culture is so youth oriented, it has become harder and harder to stay in the game.

That's why I decided to write this book. Like many of you, I was divorced in my early 30s and a single parent for many years. After I was let go from a job I loved, I started my own consulting business. My parents became ill and passed away while I was trying to cope on my own with an out-of-control teenaged son. By the time my primary client's business failed in the great recession, I had been out of the workforce for more than 20 years. At each turn, I was forced to reinvent myself – and find new clients and new businesses. How did I do it? By reinventing myself over and over. I was fortunate enough to meet and marry a wonderful man. I became a licensed Realtor®, a certified resume writer, and a real estate investor with a number of rental properties that I manage. My husband calls me "Leona." I also started to write e-books, and now I am publishing them in paperback.

As a result of my personal experiences, I have come to the conclusion that reinvention is your only option. You almost have to reinvent yourself every 7 or so years if you are going to stay relevant and "in the game." Although men also face problems with aging, I believe it is worse for women. We are pulled in more directions, and we take things much more personally. That's why it is so important to keep current with technology and up-to-date with your personal appearance. You also need to eat right and stay active in order to maintain your health and energy.

There isn't a woman in America who isn't flattered to be carded in a restaurant or mistaken for someone years younger. Aging isn't just about gray hair and wrinkles. It's how you carry yourself, your self-image, and your confidence. If you look and feel great and you have kept up with marketable skills, you can stay in the game and take on whatever comes your way.

I hope you will enjoy this book and profit from the many tips I have assembled to help you look and feel your best. And don't forget continuing education. Life is moving at a tremendous clip, and you need to stay up-to-date with computers, smart phones, the Internet, and contemporary culture if you want to stay in the game.

So here's to you...loose that 10 pounds. Join a gym or begin an exercise program. Update your wardrobe and get a new haircut. Look younger, feel better, live longer. Stand tall and let the world hear you roar!

Whitney Smith
West Chester, PA
2015

Chapter 1: Understand Your Skin to Help Reverse the Signs of Aging

Your skin is made up of 3 layers: the Epidermis or outer layer, Dermis or middle layer and Hypodermis, the under or fatty layer. When you understand the purpose and function of each of these components, you can do what is necessary to stimulate the growth and renewal that is necessary for a younger looking you.

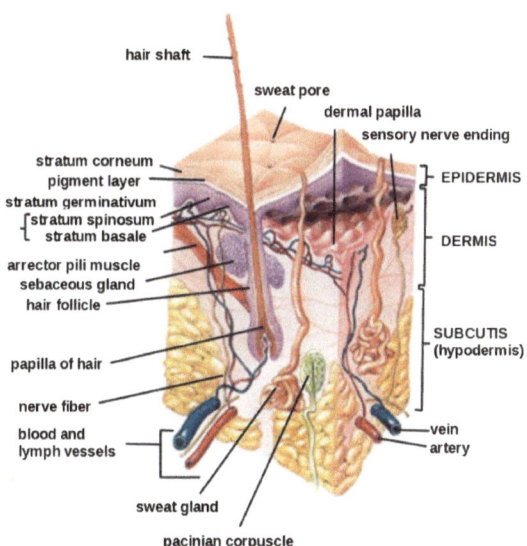

From the time you are born until you reach your mid 20's, your skin works like it was designed to. Then, at about age 25, the skin's natural regeneration process starts to slow down. Old dead cells in the Epidermis are replaced more slowly. The surface skin cells take longer to turn over and wounds take longer to heal.

After age 45, it gets even worse. The skin begins to thin due in large measure to a drop in hormones that occurs with menopause. This causes the skin to lose strength and elasticity. It becomes dryer and sagging begins.

The lower layer or Hypodermis is primarily composed of fat and is designed to provide heat insulation and shock absorption. As you get older, the Hypodermis layer loses fat and becomes less plump and smooth. Wrinkles start to form. Cheeks hollow out, jowls begin to form. And the numbers of blood vessels decrease – causing your skin to lose youthful color and glow. To make matters even worse, gravity is at work, pulling on your weakened skin and causing sagging and aging.

Here's what you need to do the combat the natural aging process: The skin completely replaces itself about once each month. It takes longer as we grow older. The Epidermis or outer layer is composed of hard, flattened dead cells that form a protective layer. The outermost layer is constantly shedding dead cells which are being replaced by newer cells that are generated in the Dermis, then pushed up from below. When this process slows down with age, dead cells accumulate on the skin's surface and your skin becomes dull and lifeless.

The Dermis is a dense network of specialized cells: collagen which provides the skin's structure; elastin which gives skin its elasticity and the ability to stretch and regain shape; and fibroblasts which synthesize skin proteins and repair the skin. The cells in the Dermis are plump and round, full of moisture. As they are pushed toward the surface, they become flattened and lose most of their water content.

What should you do to reverse the signs of aging and regenerate your skin? The most important steps in your skincare regime are cleansing and exfoliating. You need to be sure to clean your skin thoroughly every night, because if your skin isn't perfectly clean, your expensive skin products will not work like they are intended. Your skin also repairs itself overnight while you sleep, so it is an ideal time to apply anti-aging products. You don't want to use soap to clean your face – it is too harsh and will strip your skin of its moisture barrier. Instead, use a cleanser with alpha hydroxyl acid to open your pores and dissolve oily plugs. Next, use a non-alcoholic toner as a 2nd cleansing step to remove the dirt cleansers often miss.

The most important step is to exfoliate. This removes the accumulation of dead cells on the surface of the Epidermis. The more you wear this layer down, the more your skin will glow. You'll stimulate cell turnover and encourage collagen production in the Dermis. Your skin will become thicker and more resilient. When you get rid of the layer of dead cells, your expensive skincare products can penetrate into the Dermis where they are needed to promote cell renewal.

Great skincare doesn't have to cost a fortune. After cleansing and toning, while your face is still wet, use baking soda to gently scrub your face in a circular motion. Then rinse and pat dry. Of course, you can buy specialized exfoliants or scrubs but baking soda works, too. If you do opt for a commercial exfoliant, avoid products containing plastic microbeads because they have been proven to be bad for the environment.

You should cleanse your face thoroughly every night before bed – and then use an exfoliant product once or twice a week. The exfoliant should have very fine granules, not large, sharp particles like apricot shell. You want to polish your skin, not scratch and irritate it. Good options include *Dr. Denese Firming Facial Microdermabrasion Cream* ($39), *Boots No. 7 Total Renewal Microdermabrasion Exfoliator* (available at Target for $15.79), and *Olay Regenerist Microdermabrasion and Peel System* ($25.99).

You might consider investing in a Clarisonic Mia, a highly rated battery-operated sonic cleansing brush that you can use in the shower. The Clarisonic is available from QVC where it has been one of the most highly rated products in QVC history – or you can purchase it on Amazon or at ULTA and other beauty outlets. Cost: $149.99. (Watch for sales at $99.) There are other similar products available at lower prices.

After your skin has been cleansed, toned, and exfoliated, you'll want to apply a water-based serum that will penetrate into your Dermis and deliver rich peptides to stimulate your skin to produce fresh new cells. Look for a formulation that includes Matrixyl 3000. Matrixyl 3000 almost doubles the amount of collagen that the body produces to significantly reduce the signs of aging. Do a search on Amazon by ingredient to find a selection of products. On Amazon, you can compare the ingredient list of the various offerings, plus you can benefit from the unpaid reviews from people who have purchased the products.

Research has shown that after using a serum with Matrixyl twice daily for 4 months, subjects' wrinkle volume was reduced by 36% and wrinkle depth by 26% while skin roughness was decreased 13%. Try to find a product with a high concentration of Matrixyl 3000...at least 3%. Some (but not all) companies will list the concentration of Matrixyl. If there is no listing or it is not clear, call the company or check their Website.

Other products that contain Matrixyl include: *Olay Regenerist Daily 3 Point Cream* and *L'Oreal Paris Collagen Filler Lip Treatment* available in drugstores and *Boots No.7 Protect & Prefect Intense Beauty Serum* available at Target.

Next, you need to build up your skin with a lipid or fat-based creamy moisturizer to retain water and restore your skin lipid barrier. You want something with bioidentical lipids or ceramides. Avoid mineral oil and lanolin.

Lipids are essential components of skin and play a crucial role in the skin's barrier function. They are found in 2 places: cell membranes of skin cells where they form what is known as a lipid bilayer and in the intercellular matrix -

the glue that holds cells together in the Stratum Corneum – the outermost layer of the epidermis that consists of dead cells. Damage to intercellular lipids weakens the skin's barrier function, and that leads to irritated, inflamed, red, dry, flaky, rough skin. *Elizabeth Arden Ceramide* products and *Olay Regenerist Micro Sculpting Cream* are 2 good choices.

Finally, don't forget your sun protection. Too much sun exposure is the number one cause of premature skin aging. Apply sunscreen daily with at least SPF 15, but SPF 30 is better. People who use sunscreen daily show 24% less skin aging than those who do not use sunscreen daily.

Chapter 2: 21 Habits of Women Who Look Younger Than They Actually Are!

Some women look young and vital at every age. What are their secrets? If you are constantly being mistaken for someone much older than you are, here are some easy, low-cost or no-cost things you can do to turn back the hands of time!

#1: They Protect Their Faces From Sun Exposure!

The single WORST thing you can do to your skin is over-expose it to the sun. The sun's damaging UV rays cause oxidation that results in wrinkles, age spots, uneven skin tone, and several forms of skin cancer. In fact, as much as 80 – 90% of aging is due to environmental damage, so protect your precious skin from the sun.

Worse yet is the danger of skin cancer. Each year in the US, nearly 5 million people are treated for skin cancer. There are more new cases of skin cancer each year than the combined incidences of breast, prostate, lung, and colon cancer. Over the past 3 decades, more people have had skin cancer than all other cancers combined. In fact, 1 in 5 Americans will develop skin cancer in the course of a lifetime.

The good news is that skin cancer doesn't need to be fatal. The average survival rate with melanoma increased from 49% in the 1950s to 91% today. If the melanoma is detected early (before the tumor has spread to regional lymph nodes or other organs) survival rate is about 98%. The survival rate falls to 63% when the cancer spreads to lymph nodes and 16% when it metastasizes to distant organs.

Always use broad spectrum sun block to protect against both UVA and UBA rays with a minimum of SPF 15. Use it all day, every day, even when it is raining or in winter. Be especially diligent about sunscreen if you ski, because sun reflecting off the snow can cause a nasty burn.

For best results, use a day cream that has been formulated with a sun block, and start today so you won't do any more damage. In the summer and on vacation or on the ski slopes, increase the SPF to 30 or above.

Today's sunscreens contain many additional anti-aging extras such as antioxidant vitamins and moisturizers, but the most important ingredient is the SPF – so the basic option is just as good as a more expensive version with lots of additives. For everyday use, try the BB and CC creams and foundations that are formulated with SPF 15 or 20. Every major beauty line has a version, even the drugstore varieties.

If you have sensitive skin that reacts to the chemicals in sunscreen, try a mineral sunscreen that contains zinc or titanium oxide. These create a barrier to reflect light away without being absorbed into your skin. And don't forget your neck – the skin there is thinner than on your face, and it ages more quickly.

However, do not avoid sunlight altogether. Our bodies need Vitamin D, also called the sunshine vitamin. It is produced by sunlight falling on the skin, then absorbed and circulated in the blood stream. Vitamin D enhances all vital organs and reduces the risk of cancer throughout the body. Low Vitamin D levels increase the risk of cardiovascular disease and mental depression as well as osteoporosis. More on Vitamin D in later sections.

Therefore, it is advisable to get moderate amounts of sun exposure unprotected by clothing or sunscreen on a regular basis. This does not mean you should sit in the sun until your skin turns red – or that you should indulge in tanning in the middle of the day when the sun is at its hottest.

Don't shower or bathe before taking your therapeutic sunbath. Your skin's natural oils will help protect it. After sunbathing, these oils need to be absorbed into the skin, so don't shower for an hour or two after sun exposure either.

To be on the safe side, you should also take a Vitamin D3 supplement to be sure your are not deficient in this important vitamin.

#2: They Have Stopped Smoking.

Next to sun worshiping, smoking is the single most detrimental thing you can do for your skin. Besides being enormously dangerous for your overall health, smoking ages the face, hands, and body, causes broken blood vessels, enlarged pores, pigmentation spots, lines around the mouth, crow's feet, a dull complexion, loss of elasticity, and wrinkles.

For every 10 years you continue to smoke, the face of a 20-a-day smoker ages 14 years. That means if you started smoking in your teens, by the time you are in your 40s, you could have as many wrinkles as a non-smoker in her 60s.

Smoking reduces the production of collagen by up to 40%. Collagen is the protein found in our skin which keeps it plump and springy. When we are young, our bodies produce sufficient amounts of collagen, but as we age production slows. Smoking causes collagen production to decline by 40% more than normal aging, greatly speeding up the aging process. The accumulation of nicotine in your body also deprives your skin cells of vital oxygen, and it reduces blood flow to the skin, robbing it of even more nutrients.

It gets worse. Smoking damages nerve endings in the skin, causing sensitivity. It has a drying effect on the skin which causes dehydration that leads to wrinkles. Plus, smokers squint and pucker while they smoke, and that creates what cosmetic surgeons call "smoker's face," wrinkles and lines around your mouth and eyes that identify you as a smoker.

And worse. Smoking reduces the body's supply of Vitamin A which protects against skin damage and Vitamin C which protects against free radicals and premature aging.

Everyone knows it is extremely hard to stop smoking, but the benefits are almost instant when you do. Within 8 hours, nicotine and carbon monoxide levels in your body are cut in half. In just 2 weeks, you'll see an obvious improvement in your skin's texture and color – no more dull, yellowish gray.

So…if you are serious about looking younger than your age and you smoke or hang around with others who smoke, it's time to STOP!

#3: They Avoid Tanning Beds!

Tanning beds are NOT a safer way to tan and should be avoided at all costs. In fact, the

UVA rays used by tanning salons cause the MOST skin damage, penetrating deep into your skin to break down the collagen that forms the structure of your skin.

Research has shown that those who use tanning beds are at higher risk for developing skin cancers like basal cell carcinoma, malignant melanoma, and squamous cell carcinoma (the most common form of skin cancer). More people develop skin cancer because of tanning than develop lung cancer because of smoking. In addition, tanning beds may be linked to eye disorders like macular degeneration and cataracts.

If you absolutely cannot live without a tan – you feel pale and washed out – try a self-tanner. You don't have to spend a fortune either. Try *Jergen's Natural Glow* which is just about $4 and available in drugstores and groceries. It works gradually, so use it daily after your shower. For an extra glow, apply *Palmer's Cocoa Butter Leg Gloss* over it. Another option is *L'Oreal Sublime Glow for the Body* which retails for around $10. Apply after you exfoliate in the shower. This is also available in drugstores and groceries.

#4: They Drink Less Alcohol.

While moderate consumption of alcohol has been shown to have health benefits, it is very easy to overdo it. Women should have no more than a glass or 2 of wine each day – and they should probably abstain from drinking completely at least 2 days each week. Alcohol raises your blood pressure, causing your capillaries to dilate. Over time, the capillaries will weaken, leading to permanent redness and sensitivity.

Alcohol also causes dehydration and destroys minerals you need for daily skin function. It generates a lot of aging free radicals and puts a strain on your liver, causing a buildup of toxins that show up in your skin as wrinkles and broken blood vessels.

Alcohol affects the production of the sleep hormone melatonin, resulting in a less than ideal night's sleep. Drink red or white wine in moderation, but avoid hard liquor because it has been shown to increase the risk of breast cancer. If you like a drink now and then, be sure to eat foods that clean and support the liver like broccoli, artichokes, cauliflower, beets, radishes, and fennel.

#5: They Are Careful About How Much Coffee They Drink.

Drinking several cups of coffee every day has benefits – like boosting endurance and delivering over 400 antioxidants, minerals, and phytonutrients including Vitamins A1, B1, B2, C, D, E, calcium, magnesium, iron, potassium, zinc, copper, phosphorous, and chromium. Choose pesticide-free, organic coffee.

Your morning Joe also uplifts your mood, enhances brain power, and has been shown to help people with depression or dementia. Researchers have discovered that people who drink 3 to 5 cups of coffee a day have a 65% decreased chance of developing Alzheimer's disease or dementia later in life.

Another study done in Japan with more than 76,000 participants found men consuming 1 or 2 cups of coffee daily reduced their risk of dying from a cardiovascular disease by as much as 38%.

However, there is a dark side to drinking coffee. If you consume more than 4 cups a day, coffee will do more than make you jittery and interrupt your sleep. A new study by the Mayo Clinic suggests that men who drink more than 28 cups of coffee in a week have a 56% higher risk of dying from any cause.

To minimize the affect coffee has on your shuteye, drink only decaffeinated coffee after lunch and beyond.

#6: They Drink Lots of Water – 8+ Glasses a Day!

Water keeps your skin hydrated and helps flush out waste toxins from your body. Did you know it is estimated that 70,000 chemicals foreign or harmful to the human body are in common use today? Plus, 1000 more compounds are being introduced each year.

That means we are being contaminated by substances that haven't existed in nature before – and the more toxins you have in your body, the older you'll look and the worse you'll feel.

Toxins are everywhere: in our food, in the air, in the products we use to clean our homes, and in the beauty products we buy. This toxin overload has been blamed for the rise in infertility, food intolerances, and allergies that are so prevalent today.

Your kidneys need about 64 ounces of water each day in order to function effectively. Drinking sufficient water helps eliminate toxins and flush fat and waste from your system.

For every 25 pounds of extra weight you are carrying, you'll need to drink additional water. If you are 50 pounds overweight, add 2 extra glass of water to your daily intake, 75 pounds and you'll need 3 extra glasses. Or use this easy formula: divide your weight by 2 to determine how many ounces of water you'll need each day to avoid dehydration.

Water also helps suppress your appetite. When you are feeling hungry between meals, you might actually be thirsty – so drink a glass of cold water instead of indulging in a snack. You can also reduce your appetite by drinking a big glass of water before every meal.

The good news if you don't really like water? Coffee and tea also count towards your daily intake making it easier to rack up 8 glasses. However, alcohol does not count as it is actually dehydrating.

Try to drink most of the water early in the day so you won't be up all night going to the bathroom.

#7: They Get Plenty of Sleep – at Least 7 – 9 Hours!

Sleeping fewer than 6 hours or more than 10 hours each night has been linked to chronic diseases including heart disease, diabetes, and obesity. Sleep helps your body rejuvenate and heal itself – and it increases the production of human growth hormone (HGH) which is produced by the pituitary gland and slows aging. HGH helps reduce fat stored in your cells and combats many signs of aging.

Lack of sleep accelerates the aging process. People deprived of sleep have higher levels of the stress hormone cortisol which slows down the skin's natural repair functions. Plus, your skin repairs itself at night while you sleep, so be sure to get the amount of sleep you need.

Sleeplessness stimulates hunger and triggers insulin resistance, interfering with how the body metabolizes fat...resulting in weight gain. In fact, sleeping fewer than 6 hours a night increases obesity risk by 30%. Skimping on deep sleep can also reduce the body's sensitivity to insulin, increasing your risk of type 2 diabetes.

Disrupted sleep not only ages you, it is linked to many health problems including high blood pressure, a compromised immune system, and depression. Getting 6 or fewer hours of sleep over the long term increases your risk of developing or dying of heart disease by 48%. And you are 20% more likely to develop high blood pressure. Not enough sleep can also cause lack of concentration, give you dark under-eye circles, and make you crabby and irritable.

Hitting the snooze button is not the answer either. Disrupting your sleep diminishes the benefits of rest, leaving you more tired than if you had gotten up when the alarm went off in the first place.

#8: They Sleep on Their Backs!

Did you know the average human head weighs more than 10 pounds? If you sleep with your face mashed into your pillow, you are bound to wake up in the morning with creases on your face from your pillow, sheets or pillowcases. When this happens night after night, you will eventually end up with permanent dents and wrinkles on your face.

You should also sleep with your head slightly elevated so the blood that accumulates in the tiny blood vessels in the delicate area under your eyes can drain away, reducing bags and dark circles. Also reduces snoring.

If you have trouble sleeping on your back, try one of those U-shaped airline travel pillows. It will keep your head in one place and help prevent you from turning onto your side.

#9: They Never Sleep in Their Makeup!

Always at least wipe it off with a disposable beauty wipe – even if it is late. A recent survey revealed that 1/3 of the women questioned confessed to sleeping with their makeup on at least 2 nights a week.

How bad is this habit? Very, very bad indeed. Sleeping in your makeup clogs your pores and oil glands. When makeup becomes impacted in your pores, they appear larger. They also get stretched out – and because your collagen levels decline with age, your pores will have an increasingly difficult time bouncing back to their original size.

But it gets worse than that. Environmental pollutants get stuck to the makeup during the course of your day, causing oxidative stress where you skin is attacked by free radicals. Sleeping in makeup also has an occlusive effect. It forms a barrier over the surface of your skin, locking in any irritants and exacerbating allergic reactions. Moisturizers are locked out.

So keep a container of baby or beauty wipes on your nightstand for those nights when you are too tired to engage in your usual evening cleansing routine. Your skin will thank you!

#10: They Always Wear Sunglasses!

Movie stars and celebrities always sport big sunglasses, and so should you. Sunglasses protect your eyes from damaging UV rays that have both short and long term effects on eye health including cataracts and macular degeneration.

Sunglasses also protect from glare and prevent you from squinting which causes aging crow's feet to form around your eyes.

A survey done in 2012 of 10,000 Americans found that less than ½ recognized the benefits of sunglasses and 27% reported never wearing them.

You should wear sunglasses year-round, because sun reflects off sand, pavement, water, and snow. Shop for lenses designed to block 99% - 100% of UVA and UBA light. Glasses that meet this standard are available at all prices, so you don't have to spend a fortune on designer frames unless you want to.

#11: They Reduce the Stress in Their Lives

Simplify and slow down so you can "smell the roses." Try to relax and unwind, particularly after a hectic day. If you are having trouble getting everything finished in your day, get up earlier to get a jump on your to-do list. Set priorities so you can accomplish the important things you need to get done – and don't get sidetracked on Facebook or Twitter. The unimportant issues can wait for another day.

To really relax, try meditation or yoga.

#12: They Exfoliate 2-3 Times Per Week

It is easy to do, and the pay-off is enormous. You can use a special exfoliating product – or try this: clean your face and, while it is still wet, use a handful of baking soda to gently scrub your face in a circular motion. Then rinse and pat dry.

This simple action will remove dead skin cells that have accumulated on the surface of your skin, revealing a brighter, more flawless looking skin. Frequent exfoliating stimulates the production of elastin and collagen which add structure and thickness to your skin. It also tightens and prevents sagging and diminishes age spots, fine line, and wrinkles.

Here's an added benefit: when you apply your expensive skin care products to exfoliated skin, your products can penetrate deeper into your skin, increasing the effectiveness so your creams and lotions work harder for you.

#13: They Do Facial Exercises

You go to the gym to work on your body to increase muscle tone and reduce sagging and bagging. Why not do some exercises that benefit your facial muscles? You can tighten up "turkey neck" and sagging jowls, lift drooping eyelids, ease nose to mouth lines, and more.

Sagging skin is caused by aging – the breakdown of the skin's collagen and elastin – and gravity. As we get older, the muscular structure that underlies the skin weakens and the pull of gravity causes skin to droop. Simple activities like standing, sitting and walking when combined with gravity will cause the skin to sag.

Facial exercises are an excellent way to improve the tone and texture of your skin. Just 10 – 15 minutes twice a day is all it takes. You can even do these exercises when you are driving in your car or sitting at your desk. Just be sure to sit up straight.

Hooded eyelids:
You can tell you have hooded eyelids if your eyeliner tends to transfer into the crease area of your lids before it is completely set. If this is something that happens to you, try these easy eyelid exercises:
- Relax your eyebrow area, then place the 3 middle fingers of each hand directly under your eyebrows.
- Drop the palms of your hands flat against your face.
- With the pads of your fingertips directly under your eyebrows, push your eyebrows upwards and slightly outwards.
- Hold your eyebrows in this position with your eyes wide open.
- Slowly push your eyebrows down against your fingertips while holding your eyebrows high, and hold the contraction for 5 seconds.
- Remove your hands from your face.
- Breathe in deeply through your nose, and exhale through your nose.
- Repeat the exercise. This time, hold the contraction for 10 seconds. At the 7th second, close your eyes, keeping your eyebrows held high.
- Remove your hands from your face. Breathe in deeply through your nose, and exhale through your nose. Begin

again, holding the contraction for 10 seconds and closing your eyes at the 7th second. Repeat the movement again so that you have exercised for a total of 35 seconds.

Lifting and firming cheeks:
- With mouth closed, press lips together and smile as widely as possible.
- Keep smiling, aiming to reach your ears with the corners of your mouth.
- Wrinkle your nose so your cheek muscles move upward.
- Hold for a count of 5. Repeat 5 – 10 times.

Sagging skin in chin area:
- Place the palm of your hand under your chin, letting your fingers lightly touch your nose.
- Open your mouth as wide as you can and apply light pressure on your chin.
- Slowly push your chin up until your mouth is closed.
- Repeat 5 – 10 times.

Lift brow and upper eyelids:
- Open and widen your eyes as much as you can without wrinkling your forehead.
- Focus on a point in the distance and hold for a count of 10.

- On release, you should feel a rush of warmth and circulation in your forehead.
- Repeat 5 – 10 times.

For more information, see www.cynthiarowland.com and www.facialexercisesguide.com. *Facial Fitness* by Patricia Goroway is also a great reference. This book comes complete with a DVD with simple step-by-step instructions.

#14: They Stand Up Straight!

Nothing makes you appear older than a slouching posture. Walking like an old person with hunched shoulders makes you look frumpy and lacking in self-confidence.

As mentioned, your head weighs 10+ pounds. By hanging it forward, you are putting a tremendous strain on your back and spine. Over time this will weaken neck muscles and make your shoulders even more rounded. It can also lead to degenerative disc disease, chronic neck, shoulder, and back pain, and chronic fatigue.

It is estimated that more than half of all Americans suffer from bad posture. The problem is aggravated if you sit at a desk all day – or if you are addicted to your iPad or mobile device. You should avoid sitting for more than

20 – 30 minutes at a time without getting up and moving.

Another strategy: the shoulder roll

Shoulder rolls can be performed anywhere, seated or standing. As you take a slow, deep breath, count to 5 seconds while raising your shoulders. Then, slowly exhale and count to 5 seconds while lowering your shoulders. Finish by squeezing your shoulder blades together and count for another 5 seconds. You should perform 7 – 15 shoulder rolls at a time working up to at least 40 shoulder rolls a day.

To determine if you have bad posture, take the "tape test." Place a piece of masking tape vertically down the center of a full-length mirror. Then place a piece of tape horizontally from one side of the mirror to the other at your shoulder height. Add another horizontal tape at your pelvic level. Stand as you normally stand in front of the mirror placing yourself in the center. Does your head tilt to one side? Is one hip higher? Is one shoulder higher? If you answered "Yes" to any of the questions, your posture needs work.

Bad posture is also linked to arthritis, digestive problems, repetitive strain injuries, and sciatica. By standing tall, you can add up to 2 inches to your height and look 5 – 10 pounds lighter. You also reduce your bust by a least a cup size when your slouch.

To improve your posture, you need to strengthen your "core" muscles. Try Yoga or Pilates for best results.

#15: They Have Updated Hairstyles.

Keeping the hairstyle from your "Glory Days" can be very aging. The most unflattering style for an older woman is long, straight hair with a middle part. If you like long hair, part it on the side and cut layers to add softness around your face. Or wear it up or in a ponytail or braid.

Most stylists agree that side-swept bangs and hair no longer than your shoulders will take years off your looks.

A soft, layered style that frames your face is very flattering. Avoid a bob that stops at your chin – this will emphasize sagging jowls. Choose a cut that ends either above or below your jawline.

Visit your hairdresser regularly. "Bedhead" looks edgy when you are 20, not so much if you are 40 of more. Keep your roots covered and your style trimmed and shaped.

Never, ever have hair that reaches past your elbows after age 35.

#16: They Dress for Their Age and Body Shape.

Mini-skirts and other extreme styles are for the young – not necessarily the young at heart. You need to be sensible when choosing clothes. Pick items that emphasize your strengths and hide your weaknesses but help you look stylish and sophisticated.

Black, gray and other dark neutral colors are slimming – but they also make you look older. Wear bright colors for a more youthful, fun, vibrant look. Energize your dark outfits with a bright scarf up near your face. Try to dress in one color from shoulder to hem. It elongates your look and makes you look slimmer. More on age appropriate dressing in Chapter 10.

When you look better and people are complementing you, you have more confidence, you stand up straighter, and you look younger!

#17: They Are Cheerful and Optimistic!

Your facial expressions say a lot about you. If you look hopeless and discontented – or angry and mean – it takes a toll on even a young face. Remember what your mother always said – don't scowl or frown because your face will freeze that way. Over the years, a constant grim expression carves itself into your face giving you forehead wrinkles, those parallel lines between your eyes, and deep lines running from your nose to mouth. A bright, sunny outlook will help you remain young-looking for many years.

#18: They Limit the Amount of Sugar in Their Diets.

A recent European study showed that high blood sugar levels make people look older, and diabetics look oldest of all. Another study indicated that you could age yourself by 4.6 years just by drinking 20 ounces of soda every day. Researchers discovered that soda drinkers had shorter telomeres – the protective units of DNA on chromosome ends associated with aging – similar in length to those of people who smoke regularly.

Scientists theorize that the aging effect is due to buildup of sugar sticking to the skin proteins collagen and elastin (building blocks of your skin) that keep skin supple. This is also called glycation. More on this later in Chapter 6.

Others believe that glucose or blood sugar hampers insulin production which may play a role in aging. Every time you eat sugar, your pancreas produces insulin to counteract it. When the pancreas is overworked, it leads to insulin resistance (precursor to diabetes), and the pancreas slows insulin production significantly. Diet and exercise then need to be addressed to avoid developing diabetes.

The blood sugar in your blood is affected by the sweets in your diet as well as high glycemic carbohydrates like pasta and white bread. The glycemic index is determined by the level at which food elevates your blood sugar. Foods with a glycemic index value of 70 or more have a high glycemic value and should be limited in your diet.

Low glycemic foods include whole grain cereals like steel cut oatmeal and fresh fruits and vegetables (with the exception of corn and potatoes). Avoid foods that are refined or overly processed like white bread and sugary baked goods and treats.

Inflammation has also been associated with a diet high in glycemic index foods. Inflammation is the body's response to harmful stimuli and is part of the body's immune system. Chronic inflammation can eventually cause diseases and conditions including some cancers, heart disease, rheumatoid arthritis, atherosclerosis, periodontitis, and hay fever. At less serious levels, it can lead to broken capillaries, loss of skin elasticity, and breakdown of cells – all leading to fast-tracked aging. More in-depth information about inflammation in Chapter 5.

Giving up sugar and other high glycemic foods can make you look as much as 10 years younger over several months. As mentioned, sugar hastens the degradation of elastin and collagen, skin's building blocks. Sugar attacks these vital skin proteins, making them less elastic and more brittle. As they break down, your skin starts to sag and wrinkle, and you look older.

Prevention Magazine reports that many Americans consume as much as 130 pounds of sugar each year – often without knowing it. In fact, American sugar consumption has increased 40% since the 1970s.

How is this possible? Food processors and manufacturers have loaded many even "healthy" foods with sugar which often masquerades under dozens of different names like high fructose corn syrup (the worst offender), dextrose, maltose, or sorghum. Even if you are diligent about checking labels, you might not realize just how much sugar you are ingesting.

All this added sugar actually affects the chemistry in your brain and stimulates your appetites and cravings. Sugar is like heroine. The more you eat, the more you have to have.

The worst sugar culprits in the modern American diet are sodas and other sugary drinks like flavored waters, sweetened ice teas, lemonades and other fruit juices, fancy coffees, and energy drinks. A 12-ounce regular Coke contains 38 grams of sugar which is the equivalent to 9 teaspoons! (1 teaspoon = 4.2

grams.) The American Heart Association recommends that women limit their intake of sugar to 6 teaspoons or 24 grams a day. Ideally, we should eat no processed sugars at all – sugar should come from a whole food diet of grains, vegetables, colorful fruits, and berries.

But there's more. Almost all processed foods contain added sugar to make them taste good – another reason you can't seem to stop eating them. When manufacturers remove fat or gluten from their recipes, they often add in lots of sugar to make their products more palatable.

Breakfast cereals, fruited yogurts, pasta sauces and salsas, ketchup, pre-packaged meals, granolas, breads, and crackers...the list goes on and on. Even so-called healthy foods like Dannon fruit-on-the-bottom yogurt and Quaker Apple, Cranberry and Almond Granola have 13 grams of sugar each, half of the daily recommended amount. Begin to be more diligent about what you put into your mouth.

#19: They Know the Awful Truth About Artificial Sweeteners...

If you think switching to diet sodas and using artificial sweeteners is the answer, think again. Even though these products usually have zero calories, they are still dangerous! Chemical sweeteners are as much as 7,000 times sweeter than ordinary table sugar – and research has linked them to an increased risk of obesity, heart disease, and type 2 diabetes. In fact, studies have shown that people who drink 2 diet sodas a day or more had waist circumferences that were **70% larger** than the non-drinkers. Artificial sweeteners appear to disturb the body's ability to recognize calories, causing metabolic disruptions. Thus, they often end up actually encouraging weight gain, not weight loss.

So, whether you drink diet or regular soda, you are putting yourself at equal risk for weight gain and associated disease. The answer? Drink plain old-fashioned water!

#20: They Avoid Low-Fat Diets!

The low-fat craze started in the 1990's, and Americans have been getting fatter ever since. Today we are fatter, sicker, and more addicted to sugar and carbs than ever before. When food processors remove the fats from foods, they add sugars to make the foods taste better. It has been a disastrous trade-off.

Fats are not the enemy – quite to the contrary. Fats are necessary to help your body generate the power hormones like Testosterone which is composed of cholesterol and dietary fat.

People on low-fat diets often look terrible – drawn, gaunt, and weak. They are often sick, sometimes to the point of breaking down. And they can never enjoy the pleasures of a great meal – either at home or out at a restaurant.

Obesity-related health conditions include: hypertension, heart disease, congestive heart failure, stroke, type 2 diabetes, certain cancers – some of the leading causes of preventable death. Also affected by overweight are gallstones, gout, arthritis, and sleep apnea.

Some groups are more affected by obesity than others. Non-Hispanic blacks have the highest age-adjusted rates of obesity – nearly 50%. This is followed by Hispanics at 42.5%, whites at 32.6% and Asians at 10.8%. Obesity is higher among middle aged adults 40-59 (40%) than younger adults 20-39 (30%) or adults over 60 (35.4%).

What is causing Americans to be so overweight? In 1972, Americans spent $3 billion on fast food. Today it is $110 billion. 1/3 of all Americans get 50% of their daily calories from junk food. Amazingly, 1 in 4 Americans visit a fast food restaurant every single day. As a result, the average American is consuming 300 more calories a day than in 1985. There are 3500 calories in a pound. The result is a weight gain of 1 pound every 11-12 days.

Back in the day, most mothers were stay-at-home moms who prepared and served their families cooked-from-scratch meals.

Today, most mothers have careers as well – and they are harried and time-pressed. Already prepared meals and take-out are the order of the day. Added to this, food manufacturers and processors now add extra sugar – usually in the form of high fructose corn syrup – to a wide range of products.

The typical American drinks 44 gallons of soda each year. And adolescents drink more than twice the amount of soda per day as milk.

All of this has led to a sharp increase in the incidence of type 2 diabetes. In fact, 25.8 million Americans are suffering from type 2 diabetes. Worse yet, 215,000 people younger than 20 had type 2 diabetes in 2010 – and 70 million over 20 were pre-diabetic. Diabetes is the leading cause of kidney failure, non-traumatic lower limb amputation, and new cases of blindness. Diabetes is also a major cause of heart disease and stroke – and the 7th leading cause of death.

It is no wonder Americans have become so weight obsessed. But simply dieting is not the answer, because it seems like the more we diet, the more weight we gain not lose. The reason: deprivation is not sustainable long term. That means the minute you stop dieting and return to your original eating habits, you gain back all the weight you lost – and often times more.

So, what is to be done? The answer is in permanent behavior modification. You must change your attitudes about food, learn which foods are harmful and which are beneficial, and begin to understand portion sizes.

Remember, one pound is equivalent to 3500 calories. That means you need to cut 3500 calories from your diet in order to lose one pound. To lose a pound a week, you need to cut 500 calories from your intake each day (500 times 7 = 3500). If you prefer, you could cut fewer calories each day but increase your physical activity and still achieve one pound per week in weight loss.

How do you do this? Here are some valuable tips:

#1: Start Keeping a Food Diary

Get yourself a little notebook and begin writing down every single thing you put into your mouth over the course of a day, every day. You should also include an estimate of the amount or portion size of each food. Your list should include all beverages, snacks you stuff in your mouth over the sink, foods you taste while preparing meals…everything.

#2: Get a Calorie Guide

Try to estimate how many calories you are actually ingesting on a daily and weekly basis. Most people are shocked and dismayed when they realize how many calories they are actually consuming each and every day.

#3: Learn What Portion Sizes Look Like

You cannot accurately determine your calorie intake without understanding how big a typical or recommended portion actually is. You'll need a kitchen scale plus measuring cups and spoons. You'll also need to learn how to convert grams into teaspoons (1 teaspoon equals 4.2 grams). If you are like most people, you'll soon discover you are eating portions that are 2 -3 times the portion sizes listed on labels and in the calorie counting books. It's no wonder you can't lose weight.

#4: Don't Try to Change Everything All At Once

Instead, address your unfortunate eating habits one at a time. Make a list of everything you are doing that is keeping you from losing weight like not drinking 8 glasses of water a day or indulging in sodas, etc. Then tackle just one thing on your list every week.

There is an excellent book that will help you do this. It is called, *The Small Change Diet: 10 Steps to a Thinner, Healthier You* by Keri Gans. It is available in paperback from Amazon for just $6. Ms. Gans recommends that you make just one small change and stick to it for at least a week or until it becomes second nature. Then move on to the next.

#5: Create a Healthy Eating Schedule

Don't skip meals. Eat breakfast, lunch, and dinner every day plus two small snacks. When you eat every 3 or 4 hours, you will be less likely to over-indulge at the next meal or eat the wrong foods because you are starving. Plus, you will begin to boost your metabolism.

#6: Brighten Your Plate

Build all your meals with colorful, low-calorie fruits and vegetables: red and purple berries, orange carrots, green and red peppers. Half of your plate should be veggies – especially at dinner. Eat fruits for dessert.

#7: Think Before You Drink

Don't waste calories on sugary drinks with no nutritional value. Also avoid diet drinks –

they ultimately won't help you lose weight. Drink water or green tea instead. Cut back on alcoholic beverages, too.

However, you can have a little wine with dinner – but no more than 2 four ounce glasses. A 2010 study from Brigham and Women's Hospital in Boston which followed more than 19,000 women for an average of 13 years found that those who had 1-2 alcoholic drinks daily put on fewer pounds than non-drinkers and heavy drinkers. Weight gain was lowest among wine drinkers. Researchers found that women who sipped a glass or 2 of wine consumed fewer calories – and that women burn more calories after drinking than men do.

#8: Carbs Are Not the Enemy

But not all carbs are created equal. Choose high-fiber carbs but watch those portion sizes. Start paying attention to how much sugar you are ingesting. Read food labels and particularly watch out for and avoid high fructose corn syrup.

#9: Fats are Not the Enemy Either

Eating fat doesn't make you fat – but you need to be sure you're eating the right kinds of fat and in the right proportion. Limit saturated fats (contained in meat and dairy products) and the amount of processed fats you eat. More about this later in Chapter 5.

#10: Go Easy on the "Extras"

Ask for sauces and salad dressings on the side. Learn to make your own healthy and delicious salad dressings with olive oil, vinegar, and Dijon mustard.

#11: Change Up Your Meat Menu

Eat less high-fat beef. Forgo fried meats, chicken, and fish – grill, broil or roast them instead. Eat more fish. Remove the skin from chicken. Avoid processed meats like hot dogs, sausages, bacon, etc. Try to have at least one meatless meal per week like stir-fried vegetables.

#12: Tame Your Sweet Tooth and Go Easy on the Table Salt

Be aware of the hidden sugar in most processed foods. Choose items that have only 4 or 5 ingredients listed on the label. My favorite example of this is original Triscuits. Ingredients: whole grain soft white wheat, soybean oil, sea salt. Avoid artificial colors and preservatives.

Don't use iodized table salt – it is bleached white and full of chemicals to prevent caking. Opt for all natural sea salt instead. My personal favorite is Himalayan Pink Crystal Sea Salt which contains a full spectrum of 84 minerals and trace elements including iodine that your body needs. It is unrefined, unprocessed "raw" salt that is hand-mined from salt caves that were formed 250 million years ago as ocean salt settled into geologic pockets around the earth. If you have high blood pressure or eat a lot of salty processed foods, stop eating salty snack chips and canned soups, and start adding natural sea salt to your menus.

#13: Have a Plan for Special Events

Make special occasions more about socializing and less about food. Don't use vacations, holidays, and other events as an excuse to overeat. Always have an eating plan before a party – and eat something healthy before you go so you won't be starving and load up on no-no's at the event.

#14: Step Up Your Physical Activity

Try to devote 30 minutes, 5 days a week to a brisk walk or other workout. Park your car further away from your destination. Always take the stairs. Give Yoga or Pilates a whirl. There are studios opening all over the country.

#15: Always Start Your Day with a Healthy Breakfast

Studies show that people who routinely skip breakfast are **450%** more likely to become obese. Eating breakfast jump starts your metabolism for the day – and helps curb your appetite so you don't overeat later in the day.

For an easy, low-calorie, nutrition-packed meal, try this: Add a handful of whole almonds to 1 cup of plain whole milk yogurt. Top with blueberries and sliced strawberries or other fresh fruit. Calories: less than 200.

Yogurt adds probiotics to your diet to aid in digestion and enhances your immune system. Almonds add fiber and bulk. Fresh fruit is a source of Vitamin C plus fiber. You will find this to be satisfying and delicious.

#16: Effective Dieting Starts at the Grocery Store

Don't buy the stuff that will tempt you to snack and overeat. If "no-no" snacks like cookies and chips are not within your reach, you'll have to eat something else that won't wreck your diet plan like fresh fruit, carrot sticks, nuts, or celery.

#17: Downsize Your Plate

Instead of a 12" dinner plate, fill a 9" salad plate. If you are still hungry when you've finished, wait 20 or 30 minutes before you have seconds. This allows your brain time to catch up with your stomach. Or have a cup of green tea or a glass of sparkling water.

#18: Serve Food on Plates from the Stove

Do not place bowls and serving plates heaped with food onto the dinner table. Instead, ladle the food out of pots and pans in appropriate serving sizes right at the stove. Immediately pour leftovers into containers to store in the fridge.

#19: Chew Food More Thoroughly

Eat slower and really savor what you are putting in your mouth. It takes up to 20 minutes for your brain to get the message that you've had enough. Relax and really enjoy your meals.

#20: Make Mealtime a Special Occasion

Set the table with pretty placements and napkins. Add candles and a centerpiece. Serve sparkling water in attractive glasses. Never eat your dinner over the sink and avoid mindless eating in front of the TV.

#21: Get Plenty of Sleep

Those who are sleep deprived have a harder time burning calories.

#22: Order Your Burgers Without Cheese...

And save 100 calories or more. If you only eat the top or bottom of the bun, you'll save 50 - 60 more calories. Tell the waiter to hold the fries – or substitute a mixed salad (dressing on the side) and save even more.

#23: Switch to Thin Crust Pizza

And skip the high fat, high calorie toppings like sausage, extra cheese, and pepperoni. Order veggie pizza instead.

#24: Avoid White Foods

Pasta, rice, potatoes, bread, and sugar. And don't eat chips or cookies out of the bag or box. Look at the portion size, count out that many and put the rest away for later.

#25: Don't Go On Restrictive or Fad Diets

They lead to cravings and binges. Instead, try to eat less every day through portion control and make healthier food selections.

#26: Order the Small Size of Everything…

When dining out or in the drive-thru, don't be tempted to "super-size."

#27: Use Cooking Spray Instead of Butter or Oil…

When you are frying and save 100 or more calories.

#28: Skip High-Calorie or Fattening Salad Toppings…

Like bacon bits, croutons, and cheese. Try oil & vinegar instead of bottled dressings that can be loaded with hidden sugars and calories – plus artificial colors and preservatives. Always ask for dressing on the side.

#29: Avoid Sugar Substitutes.

Rats fed sugar alternatives like zero-calorie saccharin eventually gained more weight than those fed actual sugar. Scientists speculated that because fake sugar doesn't come with additional calories, the confused digestive system fails to burn calories and regulate food intake the way it would with actual sugar. Instead of the chemical sugar substitutes, opt for Truvia which is a natural substance derived from the Stevia plant.

#30: Take Vitamin C and D3 Plus DHEA Supplements…

To help your body burn fat. DHEA has been found to help mature adults metabolize sugar.

#31: Drink 8 oz. of Water + 1 oz. Apple Cider Vinegar...

Before every meal to help suppress your appetite.

#32: Have Your Thyroid Checked

An under-active thyroid can make losing weight hard or impossible. Women, especially those older than 60, are more likely to have developed hypothyroidism over time. Untreated hypothyroidism can cause obesity, joint pain, infertility, fatigue, sensitivity to cold, impaired memory, and more. Thyroid hormones have an enormous impact on your health affecting all aspects of your metabolism.

Hyperthyroidism is easy for your doctor to detect and treat. He will order a simple blood test that measures the levels of thyroid hormones in your blood. If you test low, he will prescribe a synthetic thyroid hormone, usually Levothyroxine or Synthroid. Both cause virtually no side effects and are relatively inexpensive.

#33: Only Weigh Yourself Once a Week

If you weigh yourself every day, you are going to see fluctuations in your weight caused principally by daily water differences. You will start to make yourself crazy. Therefore, only weigh yourself once a week – and keep your weigh-ins consistent. Use the same scale, the same day of the week, the same time of the day. The best strategy is to weigh yourself first thing in the morning before you eat or drink anything – and weigh yourself in the buff. Studies indicate that most people weigh less on Wednesday – so make Wednesday your weigh-in day.

An even better indicator of your dieting progress is your waist measurement – so measure your waist once a week at the same time as your weigh-in using the same measuring tap at the same spot – around your navel. As long as your waist measurement decreases, you are still losing fat even though the scale might not reflect it because your fat stores are shrinking. Remember, muscle weighs more than fat so if you are creating more muscle, your weight probably won't go down.

Be sure to record your weigh-in results in your food diary so you can track your progress.

Some Diet Foods That Could Make You Fat

#34: Smoothies

Smoothies containing kale or spinach with added fruits to make them palatable often end up containing too much sugar – as much as 6 teaspoons or more. Start the day with some whole fat yogurt with added fresh blueberries and a handful of almonds instead.

#35: Humus

Humus is delicious and a crowd favorite, but it contains 35 calories in each tablespoon. And that doesn't take into account the calories in whatever you dip into it. If you are like most of us, you can't or won't stop at just a tablespoon.

#36: Grapes

A cup of grapes has 15 grams of sugar - more than 3 Oreos which have just 14 grams. And it is hard to stop with just a few grapes. Rather you're likely to down an entire bunch which contains about 310 calories and 75 grams of sugar. Remember 4.2 grams of sugar is equal to 1 teaspoon. So a bunch of grapes contain almost 18 teaspoons of sugar.

#37: Nuts

While nuts are very good for you, 1 ounce of most nuts contains about 14 grams of fat and 160 calories. An ounce is the size of a shot glass. Therefore, it is important to control the portion size. Sprinkle nuts on a salad or in your yogurt – or count out 20 nuts and put the rest away.

#38: Gluten-free Snacks

When food processors remove gluten from their products, they add in sugars and fats so that the finished product will still be tasty and delicious. No gluten but high in calories and fat - not a good trade-off. Besides, unless you have Celiac disease, gluten shouldn't be a problem for you.

Chapter 4: Vitamins & Supplements for Better Health

Although you should be getting most of your nutritional needs from the foods that you eat, you probably are not eating optimally every single day. If your diet is limited by any of the following, you should discuss adding vitamins and supplements with your doctor:

1) Do you eat fewer than 2 meals a day?

2) Is your diet restricted – do you not eat meat, milk or milk products or fewer than 5 servings of fruits and vegetables each day?

3) Do you eat alone most of the time?

4) Without trying, have you lost or gained more than 10 pounds in the last 6 months?

5) Do you take 3 or more prescription or over-the-counter meds a day?

6) Do you have 3 or more alcoholic drinks in a day?

If you answered yes to one or more of these questions, dietary supplements might be the answer for you. Large nutritional surveys sponsored by the US government involving thousands of people indicate there are many people who are not getting adequate nutrition from the foods they eat. More than 93% lack Vitamins D & E, 61% lack magnesium, 50% lack Vitamin A and calcium and 40% don't get enough Vitamin C.

Older people and those who are obese, under stress, injured or suffering from chronic medical conditions many need higher levels of vitamins and essential minerals.

Here is a guide to the most important vitamins and supplements along with recommended dosages and food sources to maintain optimum health.

Be sure to consult with your doctor before taking any supplement.

#1: Vitamin A (Beta-Carotene)

Vitamin A comes in many forms – both animal and plant-derived beta-carotene. Vitamin A is an antioxidant which helps protect the body from "free radicals" which are natural byproducts of many of the body's normal chemical reactions. Free radicals can be very damaging. Vitamin A is also important for a healthy immune system, liver, and eyesight. The eye's retina depends on adequate Vitamin A to function optimally.

You can get Vitamin A from butter, cod liver oil, eggs, and whole milk. Many yellow and orange fruits and vegetables like carrots, apricots, sweet potatoes, and pink grapefruit contain substances called carotenoids and beta-carotene which are precursors to Vitamin A. Also available in dark leafy greens like kale and collard greens as well as vegetables like asparagus, beets, and wild rice. The body can make all the Vitamin A it needs if you get sufficient beta-carotene from your diet.

Recommended dosage is 2000 - 3000 IU of mixed carotenes a day. Best results occur when taken with Vitamin D.

#2: **B Vitamins**

There are 8 B vitamins and they are essential for core functions. They are: B1 or Thiamine which helps generate energy from carbohydrates; B2 or Riboflavin involved in energy production; B3 or Niacin which aids metabolism of glucose, fat, and alcohol; B5 or Pantothenic Acid involved in the oxidation of fatty acids and carbohydrates; B7 or Biotin which plays a key role in metabolism; B9 or Folic Acid which is crucial to fetal development and should be used by pregnant women; B12 which is used to treat pernicious anemia.

Like all of the B Vitamins, Vitamin B1 or Thiamine is water soluble, meaning the body does not store it. Severe deficiency can lead to a condition called beriberi, which causes pain and tingling in the hands and feet. Thiamine deficiency can cause neuropathy of the peripheral, central and optic nerves also leading to burning and tingling of extremities. It can also manifest as confusion, fatigue, heart attack or heart failure, weight loss or irritability. It is estimated that 33% of Americans have low thiamine levels – some severely so. Thiamine is found in whole grain foods but not in refined grains.

Vitamin B2 or Riboflavin aids energy production within the cells. Signs of deficiency include red, cracked lips and sore throat. Deficiency can also cause iron-deficient anemia and sensitive, bloodshot eyes. And deficiency can be a side effect from taking birth control pills. It is found in cheese, eggs, meat, milk, wheat bran, and yeast extract.

Vitamin B3 or Niacin deficiency can cause headaches, fatigue, and pellagra – a condition that includes inflammation of the skin, diarrhea, dementia, and even death. Deficiency can also cause amnesia, anxiety, and depression. Treatment with Niacin can lower LDL cholesterol and triglyceride levels and other serious diseases like cardiovascular, diabetes, schizophrenia, and arthritis. It also has anti-clotting and anti-inflammatory properties. Niacin is found in green leafy vegetables, grains, beans, meat, poultry, fish, and eggs.

Pantothenic Acid or B5 is found in whole grains, legumes, eggs, meat, avocados, and yogurt. It helps combat hypoglycemia, fatigue, depression, neurological problems, and muscle cramps.

B6 is used in neurotransmitter and hemoglobin production, breakdown of amino acids, glucose creation, and histamine synthesis. Deficiency can lead to swollen tongue, cracked lips, confusion, neuropathy, and ulcers. B6 is found in poultry, fish, organ meats, potatoes, and non-citrus fruits.

B7 or Biotin shortage can cause hair loss, conjunctivitis, dermatitis, and neurological problems like depression, pain, fatigue, numbness, and tingling. B7 helps break down dietary carbohydrates into glucose to produce ATP – the body's energy-storage molecule. B7 also prevents hypoglycemia. It is found in egg yolks, Swiss chard, liver, and leafy green vegetables. Biotin should only be supplemented within a B-complex vitamin.

B9 or Folic Acid is needed to manufacture DNA and red blood cells. It can help prevent infertility issues, strokes, colorectal cancer, and macular generation. It occurs naturally in leafy green vegetables, fruits, beans, dairy, meat, eggs, seafood, grains, even beer. During pregnancy, folic acid deficiency can result in neurological problems for the fetus.

Vitamin B12 is an essential vitamin required by every cell in your body. It produces and maintains DNA and keeps red blood cells healthy. It is found only in animal sources like eggs, meat, fish, poultry, and dairy products. Vegans should take a B12 supplement because they are notoriously deficient in Vitamin B12. Heartburn medications (proton pump inhibitors) and daily aspirin can also deplete your B12.

Oral absorption of B12 is poor, especially among the elderly. If signs of B12 deficiency are present, it is best to get a therapeutic trial of injectable, natural Vitamin B12.

WARNING: If you are taking antacids, please be aware of a recent study of nearly 26,000 patients with B12 deficiency compared with 180,000 control subjects. The study found those who took proton pump inhibitors for 2 or more years had a 65% higher risk of B12 deficiency. Those taking 2 or more acid-blocking pills per day had a 95% increased risk of B12 deficiency. If you are taking any antacid medication, consider supplementing Vitamin B12 by injection. Check with your doctor.

Recommended dosage is complicated with B complex vitamins, because each capsule or tablet contains at least 8 ingredients, all of which will vary in dosage from brand to brand. There is no specific dosage required for each, but you should look for at least 100% of recommended daily allowance (RDA) for each B vitamin. B complex vitamins are water-soluble. The body can store some B vitamins, but usually they are absorbed, used, and then excreted. Expect urine to be yellow when taking a B complex. If urine does not turn at least slightly more yellow than usual, the dosage may be too low.

#3: Vitamin C

Vitamin C is best known for its ability to shorten the duration of a cold, but it is also an important anti-oxidant that protects cells from damage when they are exposed to toxins like sun, pollution, and heavy metals. And it plays a role in the production of collagen, part of the skin's connective tissue. It is an essential nutrient meaning your body cannot manufacture it on its own.

Great sources of Vitamin C include citrus fruits, berries, melons, and vegetables like broccoli, red peppers, and cauliflower. Raw vegetables are better because heat reduces Vitamin C levels.

Recommended dosage is 500 – 1000 mg a day. Vitamin C is water soluble, so anything not used by the body is excreted.

#4: Vitamin D3

Vitamin D is often called the sunshine vitamin because it is produced by the body when the skin is exposed to sun. We need Vitamin D to facilitate calcium absorption and to promote bone mineralization, making Vitamin D essential for post-menopausal women at risk for osteoporosis. Studies have shown that women taking higher levels of Vitamin D3 experience 80% less abdominal fat because Vitamin D helps break down fat in the liver. In addition, Vitamin D reduces food cravings, prevents depression, uplifts mood, and increases energy.

Recent studies indicate that most adults are not getting enough Vitamin D for good bone health. You can get Vitamin D from fortified milk and cereals as well as from eggs, salmon, tuna, mackerel, and sardines not to mention exposure to sunlight. These days, many people do not spend enough time in the sun to get optimal exposure – and sunscreen blocks Vitamin D synthesis.

Recommended dosage is 2000 IU of D3 a day. Avoid D2 which isn't metabolized well. Your body needs Vitamin A to absorb Vitamin D, so be sure to take beta-carotene as well.

#5: Calcium

Calcium is important for optimal bone health, particularly as we age. It is also important for normal muscle and nerve function. Diet is the best way to get calcium – but if you don't get enough with what you eat, calcium supplements might be the answer.

How much calcium you need depends on your age and sex, with older people – both men and women – requiring more. Your body also needs Vitamin D in order to absorb calcium. Because your body doesn't produce calcium, you must get it from other sources.

The main source of dietary calcium is in milk and dairy products. Non-dairy sources include green leafy vegetables, broccoli, whole sardines, soy and other legumes, and nuts.

There are two main types of calcium compounds used in supplements: calcium carbonate and calcium citrate. Calcium carbonate has a higher percentage of calcium. It is also the cheapest.

Recommended dosage: Most adults need from 1,000 to 1,200 mg of calcium a day. However, you should have a bone density test or DEXA scan to determine if you even need a calcium supplement. Then you should discuss it with our doctor to see what is right for you. Excessive calcium does not provide extra bone protection. In fact, if the calcium in your diet combined with supplementation exceeds requirements, you could increase your risk of health problems like kidney stones, constipation, calcium build-up in your blood vessels, and impaired absorption of iron and zinc.

#6: **Vitamin E**

Another of the antioxidants, Vitamin E is important to your immune system and heart. It protects your body from the harmful effects of free radicals which are molecules that have an unpaired electron. Because of this unpaired electron, free radicals seek out electrons from other cells, oxidizing them and damaging them and the tissues they form. Proper levels of Vitamin E prevent blood from clotting unnecessarily, lowering the risk of heart attack and stroke. It also helps prevent LDL cholesterol from contributing to atherosclerosis.

You can get Vitamin E from nuts, seeds, leafy green vegetables, and vegetable oils like soybean, canola, and corn.

Recommended dosage is 30 IU a day. High intake of Vitamin E (400 IU) has been linked to prostate cancer so it is important for men to use in moderation. Vitamin E is also available as an oil that can be applied topically to your skin to help it retain its natural moisture content. Vitamin E oil makes dull-looking, dry skin look healthy and fresh. Also good for keeping your nails and cuticles in shape. Vitamin E oil is available in health food stores.

#7: CoQ10

If you are taking a cholesterol-lowering statin drug like Lipitor or Zocor, be aware that statins severely deplete your body's natural levels of CoQ10 which fuels your heart. After the age of 30, natural levels of CoQ10 begin to diminish. By age 50, your levels may be too low to support optimal heart function.

CoQ10 supplements are great for supporting heart health, raising energy levels, and protecting against the damaging effects of aging. Although CoQ10 supplements are widely available, not all CoQ10 is created equal. You should look for CoQ10 labeled ubiquinol because it is the fastest acting and most natural form and bioavailable – or body ready – form of CoQ10. Over 90% of the CoQ10 found in your body is stored in the form of ubiquinol. You should also make sure it is made in the USA and contains an ingredient called Kaneka QH®.

Recommended dosage is to start with 200 mg to 300 mg for 2 to 3 weeks, then reduce to 100 mg to maintain a healthy ubiquinol level.

#8: Iodine

Iodine has been called the most misunderstood nutrient. There are many myths concerning iodine. First, that you get enough iodine in iodized table salt. Second, that taking iodine will cause or worsen thyroid disorders.

Iodized table salt is a poor source of iodine – plus we have been urged by the mainstream media to avoid salt. The result? Iodine levels have fallen by more than half over the last 30 years according to the Centers for Disease Control, making the whole population at risk for iodine deficiency. As a result, iodine related conditions like hypothyroidism, Graves' disease, and thyroid cancer have been exploding at near-epidemic rates.

Iodine helps maintain sufficient levels of the thyroid hormones that regulate your weight, energy level, and mood.

Diets high in refined bakery products can cause or worsen iodine deficiency because bromine is added to flour as a dough conditioner. Although bromine and iodine are chemically similar, bromine interferes with iodine utilization in the thyroid. Iodine and bromine compete with each other - and too much bromine means iodine is released from the body. Bromine promotes the formation of goiter and is a known carcinogen.

The most common cause of breast pain is fibrocystic breast disease which affects more than 60% of women. Breasts become dense, irregular, and lumpy. Recent research shows that fibrocystic breast disease is a precursor to breast cancer. Dr. David Brownstein, an iodine deficiency expert, has found that the most common cause of fibrocystic breast disease is iodine deficiency.

To determine if you have adequate iodine levels, see a doctor knowledgeable about iodine deficiency and ask for a urinary test. Look for an endocrinologist who treats thyroid disorders at www.thyroid.org and click on Find a Thyroid Specialist. Labs that do urinary testing for iodine deficiencies are: FFP Labs (www.ffplab.org) and Hakala Research Labs (www.hakalalabs.com). More information can be found in Dr. Brownstein's book, *Iodine: Why You Need It, Why You Can't Live Without It.*

Recommended dosage is 6 ¼ mg to 50 mg per day. Sicker patients including those with cancer of the breast, prostate, ovaries, and thyroid require larger amounts. Please discuss with your doctor.

#9: Omega-3 Supplements

Omega-3 Fish Oil pills and capsules have become the most widely used supplement with sales reaching over $1 billion. Omega-3 fatty acids are polyunsaturated fatty acids essential for health including protection against heart disease and possibly stroke. Our bodies cannot make Omega 3-fats, so we must get them through food or supplementation.

There are 3 major types of Omega-3s: plant based alpha-linolenic acid (ALA) found in soybean or canola oil, flaxseed, and walnuts. And animal based DHA and EPA found in fatty fish like wild salmon, tuna, sardines, bluefish, and mackerel.

DHA is considered to be the most important of the Omega 3 essential fatty acids because it makes up a large proportion of your brain. Research shows that most of us are deficient in our DHA intake.

EPA is also important for good health – so a good Omega 3 supplement should include both DHA and EPA. On the other hand, ALA – the plant-based Omega 3 – is generally only taken by vegetarians who don't want to eat any fish or fish oil. ALAs are not an important part of the essential fatty acid equation. It is only useful to your body when your body is able to convert it into DHA and EPA. Unfortunately it converts poorly, especially when you get older.

For optimum health, you should try to eat at least one serving that is a rich source of Omega-3 fatty acids in your diet every day. This could be a serving of fish, a handful of walnuts or almonds, or ground flaxseed.

If you do not eat fish, you should consider taking an Omega-3 supplement of no more than 3000 mg/day. If you have already had a heart attack, you may benefit from a higher dose – but you should consult your doctor to see what makes sense for you.

Omega-6 fatty acids are also considered essential fatty acids, necessary for human health but not made by the body. A healthy diet contains a balance of Omega-3 and Omega-6 fatty acids. Omega-3s help reduce inflammation – and too much Omega-6s tend to promote inflammation.

Most Americans consume more than enough Omega-6 fatty acids. The majority of snack and processed foods like chips, popcorn, crackers, etc. are made with various vegetable oils, primary sources of Omega-6s. Fried foods including chicken and French fries are usually fried in high-heat vegetable oils containing Omega-6 fatty acids.

As a result, the typical American diet tends to contain 14-25 times more Omega-6 fatty acids than Omega-3 fatty acids. Most scientists feel the optimum ratio of Omega-6 to Omega-3 should be between 2:1 and 4:1. Since the average diet contains more than enough Omega-6 fatty acids, supplementation is not usually necessary.

Recommended dosage of Omega-3s: Not more than 3000 mg/day. Please consult your doctor before taking more than that. If you are trying to support heart health, look for a product that contains twice as much EPA as DHA. If your concerns are for your nervous system – eyes and brain – or recovery from depression or bipolar disorder, look for a product that contains twice as much DHA as EPA. It is also better to purchase products that contain at least 600 mg of total Omega-3 essential fatty acids in 1000 mg capsule to insure purity. Some low-quality products contain as little as 180 mg of Omega-3 per 1000 mg. capsule, making them 3 times more expensive and far more likely to trigger allergies or stomach upset.

WARNING: If you have diabetes, fish oil supplements can cause a rise in blood sugar levels and should be avoided. Consult with your doctor.

#10: Collagen

Collagen supplements can make your skin look younger by plumping fine lines and causing your body to rebuild collagen from within. In a large double-blind, placebo-controlled study, women took 2.5 g of hydrolyzed collagen peptide (brand name Verisol) once a day. After 8 weeks, researchers measured a 20% reduction in wrinkle depth around the women's eyes. Even more impressive, levels of procollagen (precursor to collagen) were significantly elevated with production up 65%.

Collagen keeps the skin resilient and joints working smoothly. It provides the structure in the tissue that connects your organs. When you pass age 30, your collagen production declines, causing wrinkles to form and bone and joint problems.

Collagen is a large molecule that can't penetrate the skin so it can't be delivered beyond the surface of the skin whether it is presented in a gel, cream, or lotion. However, the new hyrdolized collagen oral supplements break down the collagen molecules into microscopic pieces, making absorption into the cells possible.

When shopping for a collagen supplement, look for the peptides Verisol and BioCell. They are the only ingredients with studies backing up their anti-wrinkle claims. You can use powder, juice or capsules.

BioCell Collagen® works two ways. It contains a patented formula with hydrolyzed collagen type II (60%), chondroitin sulfate (20%) and hyaluronic acid (10%) in a highly absorbable form. This supplement provides nutrients essential for maintaining cartilage, tendon, and ligament connective tissue health. It has been clinically shown to improve joint comfort and mobility. The hyaluronic acid and chondroitin sulfate promote joint cushioning and lubrication. BioCell has also been clinically shown to reduce fine lines and wrinkles, reduce skin dryness and increase collagen content in the dermis that supports the skin. It promotes maintenance and healthy aging of skin and supports healthy hair and nails. It is available in capsule form from www.vitacost.com. Look for the private label Hyaluronic Acid.

Recommended dosage: Although collagen supplements are generally regarded as safe by the FDA, they do not have a Recommended Daily Allowance (RDA). Based on several studies, an appropriate dose for adults (21+) is 5 to 15 grams per day. However, Vitamin C is necessary for proper synthesizing, so you should take a Vitamin C supplement with collagen.

#11: Astaxanthin

Astaxanthin is a powerful carotenoid antioxidant 100 times more capable of neutralizing free radicals (the molecules that damage and age skin) than Vitamin C and E. It also has amazing anti-inflammatory properties. Two separate studies with women between the ages of 25 and 65 showed that Astaxanthin improved every aspect of the women's skin within 2 weeks, while major improvements to the skin's appearance were seen at 4 weeks.

Astaxanthin has been hailed for its ability to boost stamina, reduce exercise recovery time, improve joint health, enhance brain function, and provide a surge of youthful energy. And it works from the inside out to repair and heal your skin, reverse years of oxidative damage and stress, and help maintain a youthful appearance.

Found most abundantly in seafood, Astaxanthin gives the red color to wild salmon, shrimp, and lobster. (Please note that farmed salmon gets its inferior red color from dye). We cannot produce Astaxanthin ourselves so we depend on our diet to obtain it. However, to get sufficient amounts you'd need to eat a minimum of 6 ounces of wild salmon every day. Astaxanthin's purpose is to protect against oxidation damage whether caused by UV radiation, excess physical exertion, or diabetes-generated glucose toxicity.

Look for Astaxanthin with the brand name AstaREAL® which is produced by Fuji Chemical Industry Company. Fuji has sponsored more than 40 clinical studies to establish the health benefits of Astaxanthin as well as more than 30 safety studies to provide its reliability.

Recommended dosage: Most sources recommend a dosage of 5 – 8 mg a day. If you opt to take Astaxanthin, you probably don't need to supplement with Vitamin A. For best results, take with Omega-3 for optimum absorption.

12: DHEA

DHEA is a 19-carbon steroid hormone which serves as a hormone precursor to estrogen, testosterone, and other steroid hormones. Many chronic disease associated with aging appear to be related to declining levels of DHEA. Deficiency of DHEA is associated with age-related drops in energy, mood, memory, appetite, graying of hair, and some skin conditions. DHEA levels decline by more than 60% with the onset of menopause.

Recommended dosage: 50 mg/day.

#13: Melatonin

Melatonin is a hormone made by the pineal gland, a small gland in the brain. It helps control your sleep and wake cycles. It is produced at night when you are sleeping. Very small amounts of it are found in meats, grains, fruits, and vegetables. But you can also buy it as a supplement.

Like many other hormones, melatonin levels slowly drop as we age. If you are having trouble falling or staying asleep, you might need to take a melatonin supplement. It is incredibly safe with few adverse effects. Melatonin should only be taken in its man-made form. The form derived from ground-up cow pineal glands is not recommended.

Recommended dosage: 0.5 to 3 mg per night.

#13: Looking for a Convenient, Affordable, Reliable Supplement Source?

Check out www.vitacost.com. Vitacost offers high quality private label supplements as well as all major brands. They have frequent specials and sales. They offer free shipping on orders of $49 or more. And you can sign up for auto-ship so you never run out. Plus, you can benefit by reading the reviews posted by prior customers. Vitacost carries more than 45,000 different health-related products and over 2,500 respected top brands at prices up to 50% off regular retail.

#14: Convenient Supplement Chart

Recommended Vitamin and Supplement Dosage Chart	
	Recommended Daily Allowance
Vitamin A	5,000 - 15,000 IU
Vitamin B - Super B Complex	100% of RDA for each
Thiamine	100 mg
Riboflavin	20 mg
Niacin	25mg
Vitamin B6	2 mg
Folic Acid	400 mg
Vitamin B 12	15 mcg
Biotin	No recommended RDA
Pantothentic Acid	5 - 10 mg
Vitamin C	500 - 1000 mg
Vitamin D3	2000 IU
Calcium	10,000 - 12,000 mg*
Vitamin E	30 IU
CoQ10 - Ubiquinol	200 - 300 mg for 3 weeks, reduce to 100 mg
Iodine	6 1/2 - 50 mg/day*
Omega-3	not more than 3,000 mg/day
Collagen	100 mg**
Astaxathin (AstaREAL®)	5 - 8 mg***
DHEA	50 mg

* See your doctor to be tested for deficiency
** Take with Vitamin C for optimum absorption
*** When taking Astaxathin, supplementation with Vitamin A not recommended

Chapter 5: Is Inflammation the Reason You Look So Old & Feel So Bad?

What is Inflammation?

Inflammation is your body's normal healthy response to an injury or attack by germs, viruses, or bacteria. Your body sends white blood cells to your rescue when you come under attack, resulting in redness, heat, swelling, and pain at the invasion location. If you've ever had a cut get infected, you know just what I am talking about.

But not all inflammation is good. Many of us suffer from a chronic, low-grade, full-body form of inflammation that destroys the healthy balance in your body and causes aging and disease. You might not notice this condition as symptoms are subtle and sometimes undetectable. Full-body inflammation, if not addressed, causes your immune system to target your body's tissue resulting in any number of serious health problems from type 2 diabetes, rheumatoid arthritis, lupus, skin disorders like eczema, psoriasis, and acne...even cancer.

In fact, evidence exists to suggest that over time, virtually every one of the conditions associated with aging and advanced Western civilization are probably due to chronically elevated levels of full-body inflammation.

Causes of Full-Body Inflammation

Full-body inflammation can result from a toxic environment: air, food, and water; diet and lifestyle including constant high stress, too much fat, sugar, and protein; constant dehydration; too much soda and caffeine; inactivity and lack of sleep; smoking and exposure to 2nd hand smoke; refined, processed, manufactured foods instead of fresh, healthy meats, poultry, fruits, and vegetables.

A low-grade bacterial, viral, or fungal infection in your bloodstream, stomach or gastro-intestinal tract can lead to full-body inflammation. For example, you could have H Pylori bacteria present in your stomach which is almost always the cause of ulcers. Research indicates 50% of adults over 60 and 20% of adults under 40 have H Pylori bacteria present in their stomachs. If the H Pylori bacteria grows unchecked, it could result in full-body inflammation.

Chronic food allergies or sensitivities can also lead to full-body inflammation resulting in an imbalance of bacteria, yeast, and fungi in the gastro-intestinal tract, also known as dysbiosis. A typical American diet today – also known as SAD (Standard American Diet) is full of processed foods and sugar and can lead to dysbiosis which in turn can lead to "Leaky Gut."

Leaky Gut, the result of full-body inflammation, causes some very unpleasant symptoms:

1) Belching, gas, and/or bloating.
2) Constipation and/or diarrhea.
3) Indigestion, heartburn, and GERD (Gastro Esophageal Reflex Disease). Most people believe this is the result of excess stomach acid but just the opposite is often true.
4) Undigested food in stool.
5) Fatigue. Harmful bacteria and pathogens create toxic byproducts that your body must absorb and process. This leads to an immune response and causes a buildup of inflammation that often finds its way to the brain, robbing your body of the energy it needs.

#1: Adopt a Diet To Cure Leaky Gut or Dysbiosis

A diet of whole foods and lots of vegetables with the limited addition of whole grains, nuts, seeds, and fresh fruits is the best way to control Leaky Gut. You'll want to avoid baked goods, cookies, and pastries. Also foods that often cause food allergies: gluten found in wheat, rye, and barley; milk products found in milk and cheese;

soy found in tofu, soybean oil, salad dressings, etc.; sugar found in most processed foods – especially soda.

#2: Replace Your White Table Salt

Replace your white table sale with natural sea salt. Sea salt has natural trace minerals, and it comes in a form that your body can use best. It is not bleached, and it doesn't contain any chemical anti-caking agents. Natural sea salt won't be white – look for shades like gray or pink.

#3: Reduce Your Stress Levels

Stress can cause full-body inflammation, because it raises the levels of cortisol in your bloodstream. Cortisol is an important hormone secreted by the adrenal glands. It helps regulate metabolism, blood pressure, insulin release, immune function, and inflammation response.

However, high and prolonged levels of cortisol in the bloodstream result in impaired cognitive performance, suppressed thyroid, blood sugar imbalances, decreased bone density and muscle tissue, high blood pressure, and lowered immunity and inflammatory responses. It can also cause increased abdominal fat that can lead to heart attack, stroke, and development of metabolic syndrome.

Metabolic syndrome raises risk factors that include insulin resistance, obesity, high blood pressure, and abnormal blood clotting. Insulin resistance causes extra insulin to be produced which can lead to type 2 diabetes and cardiovascular complications.

#4: Other Conditions Caused by Full-body Inflammation

Alzheimer's, Parkinson's, Lupus, depression, joint pain, chronic fatigue, damage to blood vessels, susceptibility to infections, acid reflux, bronchitis, yeast infections of the skin, genitals, mouth, blood, heart or kidneys, urinary tract infections, aching back, cough, and headaches. Plus, it leads to visible signs of aging like wrinkles. Advanced inflammation can cause various cancers, heart disease, rheumatoid arthritis, and other life-threatening auto-immune diseases.

What You Can Do About Full-Body Inflammation

#5: Have a Simple Blood Test That Measures Hidden Inflammation in Your Body

It is called the C-reactive Protein Test. Almost every modern disease is caused or affected by inflammation, so it is important to find out whether or not you are suffering from it.

Inflammation unchecked can lead to allergies, rheumatoid arthritis, auto-immune disease, and asthma. Inflammation run amok is the root cause of most chronic illnesses: heart disease, obesity, diabetes, dementia, depression, cancer – even autism.

#6: The Key to Eliminating Full-Body Inflammation is a Balanced Diet!

A diet that features plenty of fresh, wholesome, organic foods. Americans eat way too much snack and fast foods resulting in an imbalance between Omega 6 and Omega 3 fatty acids. Junk foods are high in Omega 6 – so you should balance that with Omega 3 or fish oil. If you don't like fish and fish isn't a regular part of your diet, take a high quality Omega 3 supplement that contains both EPA and DHA.

#7: Aim for Variety in Your Diet –

And include as much fresh foods as possible.

#8: Minimize Processed and Fast Foods –

And try to avoid white foods like bread, rice, and potatoes.

#9: Adults Should be Consuming Between 2000 and 3000 Calories/Day

Your diet should be balanced with 40-50% high quality carbohydrates, 30% fats like cold pressed olive oil, and 20-30% lean protein. Each meal or snack should be balanced with a little of all three.

#10: Reduce Wheat Flour and Sugar – Bread and Snack Foods

Instead eat whole grains like brown rice and bulgur wheat, more beans and legumes, squash, sweet potatoes, and pasta al dente in moderation.

#11: Avoid High Fructose Corn Syrup!!!!

#12: Treat Yourself…

To 1 -2 glasses of red wine with dinner – although not every day. For dessert, have some dark chocolate that is at least 70% cocoa.

#13: Knock Off the Soda and Cut Back on Caffeinated Coffee

Instead drink 2 -4 cups of green or black tea a day and plenty of water: 8 twelve ounce glasses each day, extra glasses if you are 25 or more pounds overweight.

#14: Flavor your Foods with Healthy Herbs and Spices…

Especially garlic, ginger, turmeric, and cinnamon.

#15: Learn the Difference in Fats.

Saturated fats, unsaturated fats, and trans-fats or hydrogenated fats. Saturated fats are derived from animal products like meat, dairy, and eggs. They can also be plant-based like coconut, palm, and palm kernel oils. These fats are often solid at room temperature. They directly raise total and LDL (bad) cholesterol levels.

Unsaturated fats include mono- and polyunsaturated. They are derived from vegetables and plants. Monounsaturated fats are liquid at room temperature and begin to solidify at cold temperatures. Monounsaturated fats are preferable to other types of fats and are found in olives, olive oil, nuts, peanut oil, and avocados. These have been shown to actually lower LDL (bad) cholesterol and maintain HDL (good) cholesterol.

Polyunsaturated fats are also liquid at room temperature. These are found in safflower, sesame, corn, cottonseed, and soybean oils. These contain Omega 6 fatty acids and cause inflammation. They should be used in moderation or avoided altogether.

Trans-fats or hydrogenated fats are unsaturated but they are very harmful. They are used to extend the shelf life of processed foods, especially baked goods. Since 2006, all food manufacturers have been required to list trans-fat content on food labels – and they are being banned and abandoned by fast food companies. These should definitely be avoided.

#16: An Ideal Diet has a Ratio of 1:2:1 of Saturated to Monounsaturated to Polyunsaturated.

You should reduce your intake of saturated fat by eating less butter, cream, high fat cheese, and fatty meats. Use extra-virgin olive oil for salad dressings and food preparation. When using high heat, switch to coconut oil as extra-virgin olive oil can create free radicals at high heat.

Avoid regular safflower and sunflower oils, corn oil, cottonseed oil, and mixed vegetable oils. Strictly avoid margarine, vegetable shortening, and all products listing them as ingredients. And avoid all products made with partially hydrogenated oils of any kind. Eat avocados and nuts – especially walnuts, cashews, and almonds – and nut butters made from these nuts. But remember, nuts are high in calories – so watch your portion sizes.

#17: Don't Forget Omega-3 Fatty Acids!

Omega-3s include an essential fatty acid which means it is critical to our health but cannot be manufactured by our bodies. Good sources include cold water fish like wild salmon, sardines, herring, and cod. Also present in Omega-3 fortified eggs, hemp and flax seeds, and walnuts. If you feel you are not getting enough Omega-3s from your diet, take a fish oil supplement.

#18: Foods to Avoid

1) **Skim milk** – your body needs fat to absorb Vitamin D. Also, fat is satiating – it keeps you feeling full and prevents junk food cravings. Recent research indicates that low-fat diets not only promote obesity and diabetes, they can also cause harmful nutrient imbalances. Therefore, you should avoid all low-fat foods and drink whole milk instead of skim.

2) **Cereals** – they are high in carbs, heavily processed, and often loaded with sugar. It is also hard to control portions – a typical bowl of cereal often contains 2 or more servings.

3) **Soda** – either regular or diet. Regular soda is loaded with sugar and diet soda has been shown to increase cravings for sweets. In a recent study, people with a daily soda habit – even just 1 or 2 a day – were more than 25% more likely to develop type 2 diabetes than people who had no more than one sugary drink

per month. There are also studies showing that drinking soda is linked to accelerated aging. It lowers you pH levels which can cause acne and leave your skin looking dull and tired.

Diet soda is particularly bad because most people think of it as a diet drink. In fact, a University of Texas Health Science Center study found that the more diet sodas a person drank, the higher the risk of becoming overweight. Two or more cans a day increased waistlines by a whopping 70%. Furthermore, aspartame found in diet soda has been linked to headache, dizzy spells, and mood swings.

A University of Miami study found that people who drank diet soda every day were 44% more likely to suffer a heart attack than those who drank something else.

But soda – particularly cola – is bad for another reason. The caffeine and phosphoric acid which are contained in colas and other brown sodas interfere with calcium metabolism and building bone mass. One 12-ounce can of cola contains enough phosphoric acid to actually change the pH level in your body. The pH of cola is very acidic - between 2.8 and 3.2. The lower the number, the higher the acid content.

However, your kidneys cannot excrete urine that is more acidic than about 5.0. If your body were to dilute the can of cola to the appropriate pH level, you'd need to produce 33 liters of urine. Instead, your body starts looking around for alkalizing minerals to neutralize the acid. If you don't have enough reserves of potassium and magnesium in the fluid around your cells, calcium will be taken from your bones.

The American Journal of Clinical Nutrition surveyed 2,500 people who were asked how many soft drinks they consume. They then measured the bone mineral density levels in their hip bones.

The results showed that women – but not men – who drank 12 ounces or more of cola per day had significantly lower bone density levels than those who did not. This is caused by phosphoric acid leaching calcium from the bones over time.

If you enjoy the carbonation of soda but want to preserve your bone health, carbonated water flavored with a splash of lemon or lime is a healthier choice. Mineral water containing calcium is even better according to the Mayo Clinic.

4) **Diet foods** – sugar-free, non-fat, gluten-free. These tend to be highly processed and very unsatisfying – so you eat more of it. Many sugar substitutes cause gastric distress and bloating.

5) **Bottled salad dressings, particularly low-cal.** When they take the oil out, they add in sugar which increases calories and lessens satisfaction. Bottled dressings are also loaded with preservatives and chemicals. Opt for a simple olive oil and vinegar dressing instead.

#19: Foods that Prevent Inflammation

1) Fermented foods like kimchi, sauerkraut, yogurt.
2) Broccoli, cauliflower, bok choy, kale, and spinach – steamed for easier digestion.
3) Hemp oil.
4) Wild caught salmon, cod, sardines.
5) Tart cherries – reduce inflammation 10 times better than aspirin.
6) Walnuts and other nuts.
7) Onions and garlic.
8) Pineapple.
9) Ginger and turmeric. Reduce joint pain, lower blood sugar.
10) Olive oil.
11) Berries.
12) Peppers, tomatoes, beets – colorful foods.
13) Lemon juice – purges toxins from blood. Helps balance body pH. Improves digestion. It is a mild diuretic, and it is packed with healthy nutrients like Vitamin C.

Chapter 6: Is Too Much Sugar Making You Look Older?

Scientists have recently discovered that people with high blood sugar levels look older than their actual age. Studies found that people ages 50 – 70 with high blood sugar levels due either to poor diet or diabetes, consistently looked older than those with normal blood sugar levels. The higher the glucose level, the older they looked. And diabetics looked older still, probably because they have the worst exposure to high glucose levels.

The cause? Bunches of sugar molecules sticking to collagen proteins, making them more rigid. Collagen is a building block of the skin that helps keep the skin supple. When the collagen becomes more rigid, it reduces elasticity resulting in wrinkles and creases.

High intake of refined sugar and processed carbohydrates compromises the whole underlying structure of the skin. This is a natural process known as glycation where sugar in your bloodstream attaches to proteins to form harmful new molecules called advance glycation end products or AGEs. An abundance of sugar in your body affects the type of collagen in your skin. The common types are I, II, and III. Type III is ideal because it has more stability and is longer lasting. AGEs break down type III collagen into type I which is less stable and more fragile.

The more sugar you consume, the more AGEs you develop. The most vulnerable proteins are collagen and elastin, the protein fibers that keep skin firm and elastic. Once damaged, springy and resilient collagen and elastin become dry and brittle, leading to wrinkles and sagging beginning around age 35, then increasing rapidly after that.

Diabetics can suffer from years of undetected high blood sugar and can have up to 50 times the number of AGEs in their skin as someone who doesn't have diabetes.

There is some good news: it is never too late to turn back the clock. Here is what you can do:

#1: Build New Collagen...

With products that contain retinoids – look for retinol in OTC serums and lotions or prescription creams like Renova, Avage, and Differin.

#2: Cut the Sweets Out of Your Diet!

It won't be easy. Even whole grains, fruits, and vegetables turn to glucose during digestion. But limiting sugar will definitely help. Keep added sugar to no more than 10% of your total calorie intake. That should be around 10 teaspoons or 160 calories, the number in a 12-ounce Coke (which you shouldn't be drinking under any circumstances) or 6 Hershey's Kisses. The average American consumes 31 teaspoons per day of added sugar – equivalent to 465 calories.

Be on the lookout for sugars hidden in the processed foods you consume. Food companies give them aliases like barley malt, corn syrup, dextrose, fruit juice concentrate, maltose, maple syrup, molasses, turbinado, fructose, and the worst of all – high fructose corn syrup. The amount of sugar in each product is listed under "total carbohydrates." Even something seemingly healthy like Yoplait Original 99% Fat Free Yogurt has 27 grams of sugar per serving. A teaspoon of sugar is equal to 4.2 grams – so the yogurt contains more than 6 teaspoons of sugar!

Your skin is not the only thing affected by a diet that contains too much sugar. Sugar depresses your immune system and is the preferred fuel for cancer cells. Scientists have also found a direct correlation between cardiovascular mortality and the amount of daily calories consumed from added sugar. The highest sugar intake was associated with 243% increase of cardiovascular death.

Sugar can ruin your health in a variety of other ways as well. It greatly assists the uncontrolled growth of Candida yeast infections, it can increase the size of your liver and kidneys, increase the risk of Alzheimer's, cause hormonal imbalances, upset the mineral relationships in your body, and make you FAT by inducing abnormal metabolic processes.

Especially avoid high fructose corn syrup – believed to produce more AGEs than other types of sugars. It is a popular ingredient in soda, fruit-flavored drinks, and packaged foods like bread, crackers, and other snacks. If you are going to use sugar, make it unrefined. Or better yet, substitute xylitol, stevia, unrefined honey, or molasses.

#3: Take a Vitamin B Supplement

B1 and B6 are plentiful in food, but taking a supplement insures you are getting the recommended daily value of 1.1 mg of B1 and 1.3 mg of B6 (1.5 mg after age 50). Look for a Super B complex that contains 100% of all the B vitamins Recommended Daily Allowance.

#4: Wear Broad Spectrum SPF 30 Sunscreen Every Day

Significantly more AGEs occur in sun-exposed skin than in protected skin according to a British Journal of Dermatology study.

#5: Employ an Inside-Outside Approach to Antioxidants

Antioxidants (Vitamins A, C, and E) are free-radical fighters that help keep sugar from attaching to proteins. You can replenish your supply both by eating antioxidant rich fruits, nuts, and vegetables like cranberries, walnuts, and red bell peppers, and by applying topical antioxidants such as green tea and Vitamins C and E to your skin.

Chapter 7: Seven Most Outrageous Diet Myths

There is so much misinformation and changing information floating around that it is almost impossible to figure out what you are supposed to be eating. We've all been hearing it for years: low-carb diets are bad, eggs are bad, salt is bad, whole milk is bad.

The latest scientific research indicates that just the opposite is true. The old FDA food pyramid anchored by carbs and grains has been turned on its head and replaced by the Choose My Plate chart seen below.

1970 VERSION

REVISED 2015VERSION

So what are we supposed to be eating? Here are 7 of the most controversial foods and dietary misconceptions that have been called into question in recent years.

#1: Eggs Cause High Cholesterol

Eggs are a primary example. For years, people supposed to be in the know claimed that eggs should be avoided, especially if you had a cholesterol problem. And if you still wanted to eat eggs, you should avoid the yolk in particular because of the high cholesterol content.

All of that has now been proven wrong. Eggs have been redeemed and are now considered to be among the most nutritious foods on earth. Scientists and nutritionists now know that cholesterol in the diet doesn't raise cholesterol in the blood. In fact, eggs can often raise the "good" cholesterol – and they are high in all sorts of nutrients and antioxidants including zinc, iron, lutein, zeaxanthin, Vitamin A, D & E, and brain-boosting choline.

In fact, your liver makes 3 to 6 times more cholesterol than you can get from eating eggs and other animal products. Furthermore, your body needs cholesterol for the production of steroid hormones like testosterone and to build and repair cells.

So now, more than 40 years of research supports the role of eggs in a healthy diet. USDA, Health Canada, the Canadian Heart and Stroke Foundation, the Australian Heart Foundation and the Irish Heart Foundation promote eggs as part of a heart-healthy diet. In fact, there is no better food than an organic egg – it is the only food source that contains a full complement of essential and non-essential amino acids. Also, eggs are a wonderful source of protein and other nutrients required for good health.

#2: Drink Skim Milk, Not Whole Milk

The American Journal of Clinical Nutrition researchers have now decided that whole milk helps you lose weight while low-fat milk makes you fat. They base this new assertion on a study of nearly 20,000 women in Sweden. Researchers monitored the dairy intake for 9 years and found that women who increased their consumption of whole milk consistently lost weight (9% of their body weight on average) while women who consumed the most low-fat dairy products gained 15% of their body weight on average.

Whole milk is full of healthy fats including CLA (Conjugated Linoleic Acid), a known cancer fighter. Grass-fed, organic milk is also a great source of Omega 3 fatty acids. When the fat is removed, a high proportion of carbohydrates in protein remain, creating an acidifying affect in your body. This can cause calcium to be drawn from your bones to buffer the acid just like when you drink cola and other brown sodas.

Additionally, milk that has had the fats removed is not nearly as satisfying when you drink it. Therefore, you will likely drink more of it.

#3: Salt Increases Blood Pressure

This myth originated in the 1940s when a professor used a salt-restricted diet to treat people with high blood pressure. Then in the 1970s, research was done with rats that "proved" salt caused hypertension.

Since then, researchers have found there is no reason for a person with normal blood pressure to restrict salt intake. In fact, there is now data to suggest long-term salt restriction may pose serious risks of cardiovascular events making stroke, heart attack, and death more likely. And low salt diets are associated with poor outcomes in type 2 diabetes.

Researchers have also found that eating more potassium, calcium, and magnesium is more important than reducing salt. Potassium rich foods include spinach, broccoli, bananas, white potatoes, and most types of beans.

However, not all salt is created equal. You should avoid iodized table salt because it has been bleached and is full of anti-caking chemicals. Instead, use natural sea salt which you should grind yourself. These salts are typically pink or gray – and they are packed with natural minerals that are good for you. It is also prudent to avoid a lot of processed and fast foods that are high in sodium and low in other vital nutrients.

#4: Fresh Fruits and Vegetables are Superior to Frozen or Canned

This may in fact be true at the instant they are picked. However, the fruits and vegetables you find in the produce section of your grocery have often spent days or even weeks in transit from the farm or orchard. That means the produce was likely picked before it was ripe so it wouldn't spoil during shipment. A lot of produce is even imported all the way from South America, particularly in the winter.

During shipment and storage, natural enzymes are released from fresh fruits and vegetables, causing them to lose nutrients. By contrast, food processors quick-freeze fresh-picked produce to preserve much of its vitamin and mineral content. Canners also pick produce at the height of freshness and process it immediately.

When buying canned or frozen fruits, check the labels to be sure no sugar was added. Also be aware that the makers of dried fruits often add sugar to the product, so go easy on dried fruit.

#5: Margarine is Better than Butter

Actually, butter and margarine have about the same number of calories. Margarine, made from vegetable oils, was created as a more healthful alternative to butter which contains cholesterol and saturated fat. However, some margarines are actually much worse for you than butter because they contain trans fats which have been proven to have a more adverse effect on cholesterol and heart health. If you insist on using margarine, look for brands that have no trans fats. But why would you use oleo when butter tastes so much better?

#6: Low Carb Diets are Dangerous

Ever since the low-carb Atkins Diet was introduced in 1972, this diet has been maligned and disparaged. Instead of a low carb diet, experts began recommending a low fat diet with carbs consisting of around 50-60% of total calories.

However, low-carb diets have repeatedly been shown to lead to much better outcomes than low fat-diets. For example:

1) Low-carb diets reduce body fat more than calorie-restricted or low-fat diets even though the low-carb dieters are allowed to eat as much non-carb foods as they want.

2) Low-carb diets have been shown to lower blood pressure significantly.

3) Low-carb diets lower blood sugar and improve symptoms of diabetes much more than low-fat diets.

4) Low-carb diets increase HDL (good) cholesterol and lower triglycerides more than low-fat diets.

5) Low-carb diets change the pattern of LDL (bad) cholesterol from small and dense (very bad) to large LDL which is benign.

6) Low-carb diets are easier to stick to, most probably because they don't require you to restrict calories. Therefore, you aren't hungry all the time. However, in order to have a lasting effect, you must stick to a low-carb lifestyle even after you have lost the weight you desire. If you revert back to your old dietary ways, the weight will come right back. You must permanently change your eating habits and permanently modify your dietary behavior.

Low-fat diets have been proven to be detrimental to your health in many ways. They promote obesity and diabetes and cause multiple nutrient imbalances. The consequences of a low-fat diet include higher rates of immune dysfunction and chronic illnesses. It is best to avoid all foods labeled as "Low-Fat."

#7: Avoid Sugar Because of the Calories

Most people think sugar is bad for you because it contains empty calories and has no essential nutrients. But it is much worse than that. Sugar and its high fructose content effects your metabolism and sets you up for rapid fat gain and metabolic disease.

Fructose gets metabolized by the liver and turned into fat which is secreted into the blood as VLDL particles (Very Low Density Lipoprotein) leading to elevated triglycerides and cholesterol. And it causes resistance to the hormones insulin and leptin. That leads to obesity, metabolic syndrome, and diabetes. In fact, sugar is like heroin. The more you consume, the more you crave and need. It is without a doubt the single worst ingredient in the Standard American Diet (SAD).

Additionally, added sugar in your diet attaches itself to cells in your skin in a process called glycation, prematurely aging your skin and adding years to your looks. By far the worst offender is High Fructose Corn Syrup. However, added sugar masquerades under many names including sucrose, maltose, barley malt syrup, coconut palm sugar, dextrin, dextrose, evaporated cane juice, fruit juice concentrate, glucose, lactose, saccharose, treacle, xylose, and sorghum among many others. A lot of "sugar-free" foods have ingredients called sugar alcohols in them such as maltitol and sorbitol. These ingredients can be as bad - or worse - than sugar.

Chapter 8: Hair, Skin, Nails, and Makeup Tips

When we begin to get older, it takes more time and more money to look presentable as each year ticks by. It doesn't seem fair – but aging bodies simply require more maintenance.

As we age, we gradually add a variety of experts to our team. For weight control and fitness - a personal trainer, yoga instructor, diet plan like Nutrisystem or Jenny Craig. For health – a general practitioner, ob-gyn, eye doctor, dentist, and perhaps other specialists like dermatologist, plastic surgeon, cardiologist, etc. Many of us require hip, knee or shoulder replacements and then require rehab and physical therapy. For beauty and style – a makeup consultant, personal shopper, hair stylist and/or colorist, and manicurist.

Simply stated, getting old isn't for sissies. If we just give in and do nothing to update our beauty routines and fashion styles, we end up looking dowdy and frumpy and way out of step. So, over time we need to begin to up our games.

One of the most common mistakes women make as they get older is to stick with hair and skin routines they developed in high school and college. Your aging skin is much different than your adolescent skin was. Plus fashion trends have moved on – making you look older than you actually are if you haven't moved on, too.

HAIR

Hair might be the biggest and most obvious problem for women as they age. When we get older, our hair thins and turns gray – sometimes in our 30s or earlier. To keep your hair looking great, you want it to be thick and lustrous – plus you need a great flattering hair style. Hair coloring can make you look younger – or older – depending on the expertise of your colorist.

Here are some tips to help your hair help you look your very best:

#1: Get a New, Up-to-Date Haircut

The right haircut can take years off your looks – or make you look years older. Keeping the style of your youth can be very aging...think Donatella Versace, Ali McGraw, Jacqueline Bisset, and Liza Minnelli. Choose a classic style, not the hottest new trend. If your hair is fine, opt for a shoulder-length bob with long layers to give volume and shape. Avoid a short, layered cut.

After you reach a certain age, wearing your hair forward is probably not a great idea. A soft, layered look that frames your face is usually very flattering. Think Jane Fonda who looks fabulous! Avoid a cut that stops at your jawline as it will accent the jowls and any double chin action.

Angled, face-framing layers cut an inch below your jawline define cheekbones and camouflage a double chin. A slightly shaggy effect creates a modern, youthful look. Adding volume to the crown can make you look slimmer by drawing the eye up. The right haircut can actually make you look as much as 10 pounds thinner. Ask your stylist for a side part with side-swept bans to make a fuller face look less round.

The most unflattering style for an older woman is long hair with a middle part. That might have looked hip and with it when you were in your 20's, but it isn't going to work now. Almost everyone has asymmetric facial features. As we age and lose volume, the asymmetries become more prominent – especially if you draw attention to them with a center part. Soft waves help reverse the effect of the facial volume loss and soften angularity for a more feminine, youthful look. Parting your hair off center with a slight zig-zag tricks the eye by softening flaws. If you like your hair long, wear it up or pulled to the side with side swept bangs and soft wisps around your face.

A high pony tail brings focus to the "triangle of youth" and can be very flattering. When we are young, our faces look like upside-down triangles with the widest part stretching across the eyes – and the point at the chin. As we age, the triangle turns into more of a square as gravity pulls the cheeks down and creates shadows on the lower face, giving the face a squared off look instead of a more youthful heart shape. A high pony tail recreates that triangle by drawing the eyes up and giving facial skin a gentle upward lift.

Here are some looks to avoid: severe updo, French twist or ballerina bun…anything that is slicked back and will draw attention to every wrinkle and line. You need a soft, relaxed look with wisps and tendrils around your face. Avoid super stiff hair by limiting hairspray. Stay away from products labeled strong, firm, or ultra. Similarly, super teased hair looks dated, not retro. To get volume, use a round brush to lift hair at the root from the crown through the ends as you blow your hair dry.

Long, very straight hair won't soften the angular look that most older faces get as the skin loses fat. Straight hair also exaggerates the limp quality hair gets after years of coloring and high-heat styling. If you have tight ringlets, relax the curls by avoiding mousse styling products. Use a curl cream instead and blow dry with a diffuser nozzle.

Visit your stylist regularly to keep your new cut trimmed and shaped. Messy "bed-head" might look groovy on a twenty something in a magazine – but it isn't a look suitable for anyone over 35. Ask your stylist for hair cut recommendations – when you look good, she looks good. And be careful about the stylist you select. Consult a friend whose look you admire, and use her stylist. You should probably avoid the stylist with purple hair, tattoos, and multiple piercings. You want someone who understands the issues you are facing. African American or other ethnicity? Select someone who is a reflection of you who will understand your unique problems.

#2: Maybe Your Hair Color is Making You Look Older

The wrong hair color can drain color from your face making you look ashen and wan. Skin tone changes as we get older and our hair starts to turn gray. 50% of women will be partly or all gray by age 50. If you opt to color your hair, chances are the natural color it was when you were 20 is not going to be the answer today.

Most expert colorists recommend going a couple of shades lighter. The easiest way to hide the first signs of gray hair is with a combination of highlights and lowlights.

Any change in your skin or makeup will affect your choice of hair color. If you have developed brown spots or blotches, it might be time for a change. Think brighter, softer, lighter or highlights for a more multi-dimensional look. Brunettes usually need to go lighter because a dark color can emphasize under-eye bags and shadows. Blondes should avoid going too light – and need depth and a multi-tone color to keep looking young. And mind the regrowth. Nothing screams OLD like an inch or more of graying roots.

Thinking about going all gray? Gray hair can drain the color from your face, plus it absorbs light making your hair and skin look dull. Either dark or pale complexions look best with gray hair – sallow skins and redheads rarely find gray hair flattering. If you do decide to go gray, kick up your makeup to avoid looking washed out. Also be wary of your hair turning yellow. Use a purple or blue based shampoo or conditioner to neutralize the tone – or have your hairdresser apply a neutralizing rinse.

When you get ready to let your gray grow out, you'll need a strategy and a plan. You can go super short in a pixie cut but this is pretty extreme. Instead, have your color touched up every 6 to 8 weeks, lightening your base color and weaving in partial highlights of the pale color at the root. This will gradually expose more of your gray but it will keep it blended so you aren't showing 3" of roots.

Because gray hair is more wiry and coarse, you should avoid heavily texturized or razor cuts which will highlight the structure of your gray hair and scatter light rather than reflecting it so your hair looks shiny and sleek.

#3: Thinning Hair

It isn't only men who have to worry about losing their hair. It is estimated that hair loss affects 1 in 5 women.

There are several types and causes for thinning hair. The most common are telogen effluvium and alopecia areata.

Telogen effluvium occurs when hair follicles stop growing, lie dormant, then the hair falls out within 2 to 3 months. It is often caused by stress, trauma, or medications. Hair growth can often be restored with treatment in 6 to 9 months.

Alopecia areata occurs when white blood cells attack the hair follicles, causing the hair to thin and fall out, usually in patches. This type of hair loss may require treatment as the hair may not grow back on its own.

Your hair is a reflection of the general state of your health. If you suffer from a catastrophic illness, hair growth is often stunted to redirect energy to other cells to fight off the disease. That means hair loss is often the first sign of serious trouble.

Hormonal imbalance, emotional stress, medications, hair products, and aggressive styling can lead to thinning hair, even male pattern baldness. Thyroid problems and genetic hormonal responses to autoimmune conditions can also cause thinning hair. Hair loss is not as prevalent in women as it is in men because women have more estrogen which offsets dihydrotestosterone (DHT) that typically leads to hair loss.

It is common for women to experience hair loss following pregnancy because of hormonal fluctuations. This hair loss is usually temporary, and hair normally grows back after a few months as the hormones readjust.

Overly aggressive styling can damage your hair, causing breakage that looks like hair loss. Feel the roots of your hair – spiky broken ends will feel very different than hair shedding from the roots. Exchange your bristle brush for one with widely spaced plastic prongs or a wide-toothed comb. Use a moisturizing conditioner to help your hair retain elasticity and moisture.

Try one of the new hair oil products containing Argan oil from Morocco. This natural product assists in hair growth, reduces the rate of falling hair, helps cure split ends, and conditions the hair to make it more manageable. It is available from many makers and can be found in drug stores or online.

Try to avoid a lot of direct heat when styling your hair. That means saying no to curling irons, hot rollers, crimpers, and flat irons. If you have long hair, you should also avoid Velcro rollers which will get tangled in long tresses, causing breakage as you try to remove them.

If you notice your hair getting thinner and thinner but you aren't noticing hair accumulating in your shower drain, you should visit a trichologist (a specialist who deals in hair and scalp issues) for a diagnosis. Chances are a hormonal imbalance is to blame. But don't wait until the problem becomes very noticeable. Most problems are preventable but can be only partially reversed. To find a trichologist in your area, Google trichologist with the name of your town and state.

#4: Tips for Making Your Hair Look Thicker

Choose your hair products carefully. Select a good volumizing or thickening shampoo with matching conditioner – ask your stylist for a recommendation. Also use a styling spray or gel from the same line. Products are formulated to work together, so it pays to stick with one brand.

Or switch to mousse. It costs the same as other styling products but it lightly coats strands to add thickness and lift hair at the root.

If your hair is fine, wash it daily as it goes limp quicker than other hair types. Go easy on the conditioner or your hair could dry flatter than necessary.

Hang your head upside down when blow drying to coax volume from the roots. Dry hair in the opposite direction to the way it grows – pull all your hair to one side, then to the other, alternating until your hair is almost dry. Then use a round brush to add volume and smooth the surface.

#5: Try a low pH Shampoo

A new study cited in the International Journal of Trichology reports that your shampoo's pH is important for fixing the frizzies. Products with an alkaline or basic pH base (8 – 14) can trigger frizz by chemically roughing up the hair's surface and increase the friction between strands. That leaves your hair less manageable and more prone to breakage. Shampoos with a pH that is slightly acidic or neutral (1 - 7) smooth hair and help the cuticles lie flat. Look for a product labeled low pH or pH balancing like John Frieda or Matrix Biolage and other color support shampoos.

SKIN

Your face is the first thing people notice when they look at you – and it is the first place to show the effects of aging. In order to halt the aging process and start looking younger, you should adopt a daily routine that will keep your skin in optimal shape. That means reducing the look of lines and wrinkles, improvement in pore size, a dewy, youthful complexion that looks less dull and feels less dry, a more even skin tone with a return of youthful radiance, less sagging around the jawline and under the chin, and the reduction of brown age spots.

Let's just quickly review how the skin works. The skin is made up of 3 layers. The top protective layer is composed of a layer of dead cells. In order to restore youthful radiance as you get older, you need to continuously work to remove the outer layer of dead cells that make your skin dull and lifeless.

You also need to stimulate your skin to make more collagen and elastin – the skin building blocks that give thickness, structure, and elasticity to your skin.

If you are like most people, you are probably just washing your face at night, applying night cream and eye cream, and going to bed. Studies show that many of us sometimes even skip the cleansing and hit the sheets with makeup still in place. How's that working out for you?

So, here's what you need to be doing to restore youthful radiance, reduce pore size, and reduce the appearance of brown age spots. If your skin is sensitive, thin, and fragile, go easy on an aggressive skincare regime at first. You don't want to irritate your skin. Gradually up the exfoliation. Over time, your skin will become more resilient and it will thicken for a more radiant, youthful look.

#1: First Step – Cleansing

If you are washing your face with soap and water – stop NOW. The pH of soap which can range to 7 up to 10 or even higher will dry out your skin without properly cleaning your face. Instead, select an acidic cleanser with a pH close to skin which ranges from 4 to 5.5. You will also want a face wash with glycolic acid for exfoliation – look for Alpha Hydroxy Acid or Beta Hydroxy Acid in the ingredients list.

I personally use a glycolic cleanser with a Clarisonic Mia I Face Brush. This is a highly rated gadget that helps you keep your skin looking radiant. It is battery operated and you can use it in the shower. It runs for 1 minute, then automatically shuts off. The battery is rechargeable and it comes with its own charger - you shouldn't have to recharge it more than once a week.

Your cleanser does not have to be expensive – just matched to the acidic pH of your skin. Follow with a cotton ball soaked in an inexpensive non-alcoholic toner to remove the dirt and grime the cleanser might have missed.

#2: Exfoliating Stage

When you are young, your skin exfoliates naturally and rapidly giving you a radiant, glowing complexion. As you get older, the process slows down and your skin turns dull and sallow because of the accumulation of dead cells on the skin's surface. Exfoliating is an important step in helping you remove these dead cells.

Exfoliation stimulates cellular turnover and encourages your skin to build collagen which may improve skin thickness. Because the top layer of your skin is made up of dead cells, it is necessary to keep removing this layer so fresh new skin cells can rise to the surface. Plus, if you exfoliate and remove the top layer of dead cells, your skin is better able to absorb the expensive collagen-building ingredients in your skincare products.

You should exfoliate once or twice a week, using an exfoliating product. Look for one with very fine granules. You could try *Dr. Denese's Microdermabrasion Cream* or one by Estee Lauder, Dr. Brandt, or L'Oreal. You don't want coarse particles like apricot shell which can scratch the skin.

You don't have to spend a lot of money for an exfoliating scrub. Try one of these homemade recipes for glowing skin:

1) Baking Soda Scrub. Simply mix a teaspoon of baking soda with your facial cleanser to make it an exfoliating cleanser. Or make a paste of baking soda and water, then gently rub it onto your skin. Leave for 5 – 10 minutes, rinse, and pat dry. You can also mix the baking soda with Vitamin E oil which you can purchase at a health food store. Again, gently rub it onto your skin. Leave for 5 – 10 minutes, rinse and pat dry.

2) Granulated sugar is another natural exfoliant. Mix it with honey which contains powerful antioxidant and antimicrobial properties. Add a little lemon juice for clarifying purposes and you have a nourishing, effective face scrub. Combine 1 teaspoon of sugar, ½ teaspoon of honey, and squeeze of fresh lemon. Mix well.

3) Coffee scrub. Coffee contains caffeic acid which has anti-inflammatory effects and

can boost collagen production. To make the scrub, combine 1 tablespoon of ground coffee with 1 tablespoon of water or olive oil. Or save the wet coffee grounds from your morning coffee and use those. If you use olive oil, you can skip applying a moisturizer afterward as the olive oil will leave your skin super-moisturized. To avoid clogging your pipes with coffee grounds, plug the sink so you can wipe out the grounds or use a mesh drain strainer to catch them before they go down the drain.

4) Oatmeal scrub. This serves as a wonderful exfoliant. It absorbs and removes surface dirt and impurities, leaving your skin hydrated and nourished. Combine 1 tablespoon of ground oatmeal with ¼ teaspoon of salt to boost exfoliating properties and 1 teaspoon of water or olive oil to make a paste. Gently rub it into your skin in circular motions. Let it sit for 5 – 10 minutes, rinse and pat dry. Again, be careful not to clog up your drain.

#3: Skin Stimulating Phase

Next, you'll want to apply a serum with water-soluble ingredients that address loss of collagen and collagen breakdown leading to lines and wrinkles, enlarged pores, and loss of firmness. Please note: a cream cannot perform this function because the particles in a cream moisturizer are too large and can block the absorption of the ingredients that can stimulate collagen production.

A serum is water-based when one of the first ingredients is water and it has a thin consistency. Other important ingredients: Matrixyl 3000, ceramides, resveratrol, Vitamin C, and hyaluronic acid. You can try *Skinceuticals Serum 15* or *Cellex C High Potency Serum*. Or do a search on Amazon for the ingredients you want. You will also benefit from reading the unpaid reviews of previous customers when making your decision about what to buy.

#4: Skin Building Phase

For this step, you'll need a serum that is lipid-based to deliver collagen-building ingredients that are soluble only in fats or lipids. It will not contain any water – at least not at the top of the ingredient list. These serums are thicker and more moisturizing. Look for crease relaxer argireline, ceramides, linoleic acid, Omega 3, Vitamin A or retinol and Vitamin E. Two highly rated products to look for are *Dr. Denese Hydroshield Moisturizing Face Serum* or *Skinactives Every Lipid Serum with Argan Oil*.

#5: Skin Sealing Phase

You can select an expensive night cream at a department store beauty counter. Or you can opt for Coconut Oil or Emu Oil. Coconut Oil is an ideal natural hydrator and gentle exfoliant that helps with wrinkle and age spot reduction, strengthens the skin's connective tissue, and brightens all skin tones. Emu Oil is scientifically proven to penetrate the surface layers of the skin. If you apply Emu Oil over your serums, it helps the active ingredients to penetrate deep into the dermis where collagen is stimulated for rejuvenating results. Apply Emu Oil over any of your nighttime serums and creams. You'll be amazed at the results. Emu Oil is available online or at most health food stores.

#6: Morning Routine

If your skin is dry or sensitive and you faithfully cleanse and exfoliate at night, you can probably just splash your face with warm water in the morning. Otherwise, use your cleanser and alcohol-free toner followed by a hydrating cream. I have several stubborn brown spots which I treat in the morning before applying moisturizer and BB Cream foundation. Be sure to let each layer of product you apply dry and sink in before adding another layer.

#7: Don't Forget Sunscreen

At least SPF 15, 365 days of the year. You need to wear it all day, every day…indoors or out…winter, spring, summer, fall. I recommend the popular new BB Creams that are available from a variety of brands. BB Creams provide foundation coverage with skincare ingredients and sunscreen built in. My personal favorite is *Garnier Skin Renew BB Cream Miracle Skin*

Perfector available in grocery and drug stores for just $12.99. Then apply makeup as usual.

#8: Ingredients You Should Look For in Skin Care Products

Cleansers and Toners: Alpha or Beta Hydroxy acids including glycolic, lactic, citric, and tartaric; Vitamins C and E; Salicylic Acid to treat acne. Fruit enzymes: pumpkin, kiwi, orange, and papaya.

Exfoliants: Glycolic acid, alpha lipoic and salicylic acid, green tea extract, and Kinetin-based cream. A good microdermabrasion cream should contain mini abrasive particles like aluminum oxide or pumice. Avoid products with plastic microbeads as these are damaging to the environment. For an inexpensive alternative, use baking soda as a mechanical exfoliant or scrub. Wet your face and use a handful of baking soda to gently scrub your face in a circular motion. Rinse and pat dry.

Skin Stimulating Serums: water based with peptides like amino acid or bioactive oligopeptides; carnosine, Matrixyl 3000, Vitamin C also listed as L-ascorbic acid; alphalipoic acid, CoQ10, Vitamin B5 complex, hyaluronic acid, grape seed extract, glycolic acid to aid penetration.

Skin Building Serums: lipid based with ceramides (lipids that are identical to your skin's lipids), EFAs or essential fatty acids like linoleic acid, Omega 3, Vitamin A also listed as retinol, Vitamin E also listed as tocotrienol, crease relaxer Argireline®, DMAE, copper peptides, CoQ10, Alpha Lipoic Acid,

Moisturizers: Ceramides, EFAs, retinol, vitamins C (Vitamin L-ascorbic acid) and E, hyaluronic acid (absorbs up to 1000 times its weight in water), green or white tea extracts, Pycnogenol®, DMAE, Matryixl 3000, epidermal growth factor (EGF), Argireline®, copper peptides, Astaxanthin®, reservatrol, aloe vera, ginko biloba, Echinacea.

Ingredients to avoid: parabens, mineral oil, propylene glycol, phthalates, petroleum, sodium lauryl sulfates (SLS) & sodium laureth sulfate (SLES), DEA, MEA, TEA, triclosan, PEG, PABA, aluminum, DEET, toluene, camphor.

NAILS

Your nails can be a clue to your general health. For example, pale nails may indicate anemia. If your nails look green, it could indicate a bleeding ulcer or other internal bleeding. Peeling or brittle nails may indicate a deficiency of iron, calcium, zinc, Vitamin A, B6, or B12. Yellow nails may be caused by dark nail polish, smoking, or lung disease.

Proper nutrition can strengthen and smooth nails. Make sure you are eating a balanced diet that includes plenty of fruits and vegetables, protein, and healthy fats. Taking vitamin and mineral supplements can also help: Vitamins A, B, C, E, Calcium, and Zinc.

Do not soak your nails in water to soften cuticles. Water causes splitting, peeling nails. Instead, massage olive oil or coconut oil into your nails and cuticles. Once cuticles have been massaged and softened with oil, push the cuticle back. Do not cut cuticles as they protect your nails from infection.

Protect and moisturize your hands and nails. Keep lotion in every room of your house so you'll be reminded to moisturize. Also use gloves when you are doing household chores to protect your hands and nails.

Here are some more hints for beautiful hands and nails:

#1: Exfoliate Hands before Bed

While you are getting ready for bed, exfoliate your hands. Scrub wet hands with a baking soda paste to remove dry skin, diminish wrinkled knuckles, and prevent future age spots.

Then apply a moisturizer or massage coconut oil into your hands. If you wear beautiful rings and bracelets that attract attention to your hands, you want your hands to look great.

#2: If You Bite Your Nails or Chew on Your Cuticles...

Invest in a professional manicure. You will be less likely to pick at your fingers if you have paid good money for a professional manicure. If you provide your manicurist with your own nail polish, you will have the matching color if you should chip a nail.

#3: Consider More Permanent Nail Solutions

If you find a regular manicure starts looking ratty within days, perhaps a more permanent manicure is for you. You can select from acrylic nails, gels, and silks.

If you opt for acrylic nails, your manicurist will mix a liquid with a powder and brush the mixture onto your nails, covering the entire nail. This product hardens as it is exposed to the air. The nail is then shaped. Acrylics last up to a month but gradually your nails will grow out. You should then return to the salon to have your nails filled in. The manicurist will file down the edge close to your nail bed, then fill in the empty area. If you decide to have your acrylics removed, your manicurist will soak your hands in polish remover for about 15 minutes.

Gel nails have a similar consistency to nail polish. They are brushed onto your nails. After each coat, you must put your nails under ultraviolet light for up to 2 minutes to cure or harden the product. Like acrylic nails, gels grow out over time and your nails need to be filled in every 2 – 4 weeks. To remove gels, your manicurist will soak your nails in polish remover – or your technician may use nail-sized wraps filled with polish remover to loosen artificial nails enough for removal.

Silk nails are fabric wraps glued into place to strengthen weak nails or help cracked nails grow out. Some wraps are made of silk but others are made of linen, paper or fiberglass. The manicurist will fit the material to your nail's shape, hold it in place, then brush on the glue. Polish is applied over the glued down fabric.

These nail treatments really require a professional application. At-home products are difficult to apply – and you need specialized equipment. Be sure to ask your manicurist about proper care between visits – and return to the salon if you want to have the nails removed. Don't forget to go natural once in a while to give your natural nails a break.

#4: If You Decide to do Your Manicures Yourself...

Assemble the right ingredients for a flawless, long-lasting manicure. To prevent polish from chipping or peeling, apply one thin coat of base coat and two thin coats of nail polish. Finish with one thin coat of a quick-dry top coat. To make the manicure last, apply a thin coat of quick-dry top coat every two days.

To prevent bubbles in the polish, don't shake the bottle. Instead, roll it in your palms. Before applying polish, wipe nails with alcohol to remove any residual oil.

#5: Choose the Right Shape and Color

Shorter, well-groomed nails are more flattering on older hands than long talons. They also make it easier to perform everyday tasks like picking things up and typing. Avoid square cut nails. The best shape is a round oval. Many older women choose nude or brown-based shades of polish but these sometimes aren't good on older skin. Instead, select a strong sheer or full-blown bright shade. Many prefer the classic French manicure which looks great at any age.

For more hints and tips about nail care, consult with Louisa Graves, a noted Hollywood hand model. She has written two books: *Hollywood Beauty Secrets* and *Age-Proof Beauty Alternatives You Need to Know*.

MAKEUP

All women need makeup to look their best. Just check out the "celebrities without makeup" features in the magazines and on the Internet to see what I mean. If the most beautiful women in America need makeup to look sharp, you do, too. This is especially true as we get older and our skin loses radiance, our eyebrows and eyelashes fade to gray, and we tend to look ashy and pale. Plus, women who regularly wear makeup often have less environmentally damaged skin.

If you are still wearing the same makeup you wore ten or more years ago, it is time to schedule an appointment with a makeup artist at a department store beauty counter – or visit Sephora or ULTA if there is one in your area. Trust a professional to show you the latest products and to teach you how to use them for a great new look.

#1: Prepare Your Face

Use a moisturizer or serum. Apply a primer to your eyelids to prevent your eye makeup from feathering or creasing. If your eye makeup starts to melt after a half hour, you'll need a semi-matte primer. If your liner skips as you apply it and your powder shadows look chalky, you'll need a creamy shadow base or concealer. I now apply a concealer to my lids and inner corners of my eyes with a brush and I am loving it! Avoid your brow area as moisturizers, foundations, and concealers will cause eyebrow products to stick and look fake.

#2: Start with Your Eyes

For the fashionable "natural" eye look, you'll need 3 different neutral eyeshadow shades: a light shade to open and brighten your eyes, a medium shade to give depth to your eyes, and a dark shade to be applied to the creases and outer edges to give shape to your eyes. These colors should have the same tone. Warmer colors look great anytime and look the most natural. The lighter your skin tone, the less intense the color should be.

After preparing your eyelids with concealer or primer, begin by applying eyeliner. Choose a dark pencil to contrast against the whites of your eyes – navy, charcoal, brown, or black. No thick lines – and keep it as close to the lash line as possible. You can also apply liner under the bottom lashes – but start under the pupil and go to the outer corner. Top and bottom eyeliner should not connect in the inner corners of your eyes.

Use a densely pigmented eyeliner pencil that should glide on without smearing but shouldn't be too dry or too slippery. Liquids and gels tend to chip and flake, but experiment to see what works best for you. Gently pull your eye taut at the outer edge to smooth the upper lid for lining. Be careful there is no gap between the liner and your lash line.

Next, you'll want to "contour" your eyelids. Apply the light shadow from the lash to the brow to open up your eyes. Brush up and away from the center of your face. Next, apply the darker color to your eyelid crease and outer edge of the lid blending up to the brow bone. Use light, little strokes from the outer corner, following the arch about 1/2 of the way in toward the inner corner of the eye.

Apply the medium shadow from your eyelashes to the crease on the outer half of the outer corner of each eyelid in a triangular shape, then work the brush up the eye and blend well with your light base to add shape. For eyes that pop, the light shadow should dominate on the inner third of your eyelid, closest to the tear duct, making your eyes look larger, fresher, and more awake. The color should gradually darken from the center of the lid over the pupil to the outer edge.

To brighten your eyes even more, apply a bit of shimmery shadow or a white eyeliner pencil in the inner corners of your eyes. You can also add white liner on the inner rim of your lashes to extend the whites of your eyes and make them look larger and more awake. Then, add a highlight under the outer tail of your eyebrow on the highest part of your eye socket. You can use a light concealer or the same shadow from the inner corner of your eye. This will draw the attention up.

It is the contrast of a light lid, medium crease, and high-definition liner that makes this eye makeup look fabulous. Treat your lids to the lightest color in your eye makeup palette and never go darker than your crease color. Try a shimmer to wake up tired eyes, especially in soft neutral colors like sand, apricot, peach, honey or beige.

Be careful not to cover the eyeliner with the lid color. If you do, go over eyeliner again. You could also reinforce the eyeliner pencil with a matching gel liner. If your eyes look red, use a navy eyeliner to counteract the redness. Stay away from any liner color that is red-based – it will only make your eyes look more red.

Next, curl your eyelashes. Cup clean, dry lashes at the root into the curler, flick wrist up to curl and give 3 firm, gentle pumps. Release and repeat. To create a long lasting curl, heat your eyelash curler with your blow dryer for 15 seconds first.

Add black mascara to top lashes. Then add mascara to the bottom lashes by holding the wand vertically. Curled lashes immediately make eyes look bigger. Most experts recommend that you curl your eyelashes before applying mascara because the curler can stick to gunky lashes and yank them out. Curling your eyelashes draws the focus away from the lash line, creating a wide open look. (Remember to remove mascara each night – especially waterproof mascara. You can use Almond Oil you buy at the grocery store on a cotton ball to make it easy and gentle on your eyes.)

This "natural" look may take some practice and experimentation to get right. Every eye shape and skin tone is a little different so try several colors and techniques to see what works best for you.

#3: Now the eyebrows.

If you do nothing else before you leave the house, use some product on your fading eyebrows. Brows are essential to frame and lift the face. If your brows are pale and scraggly, it will result in you looking older and tired. Every woman benefits from elongated brows that frame her eyes. They should follow your original brow line as closely as possible. Extremely peaked brows give your face an angry or haughty look. Reshape with a softer line and lower arch.

Full, shapely, modern brows add definition, the appearance of bone structure, and attitude. They divert attention away from crow's feet, dark circles, under-eye bags, and a saggy jaw line. If your brows are all wrong, you'll look older and out of date.

Never use eyeliner pencil to double as brow pencil. Eyeliners are too soft and will smear. Instead use an actual brow pencil – taupe for blondes and highlighted brunettes, brown for true brunettes and your original shade for gray hair. You can also use a brow powder or styling gel. I just purchased an eyebrow mascara by Maybelline that I like. It is called Browdrama and comes in a variety of colors. It is a colored gel with a sculpting ball brush for easy application, and it is just $6.99, available at grocery and drug stores.

Milani makes a 3-shade Brow Fix Brow Kit that works very well. It comes in 3 color varieties – light, medium, and dark. Use the middle shade to fill in your brows – then accent with the lighter and darker shade for a natural look. This kit is small enough to tuck in pocket or purse and it comes complete with tweezers, foam pad, angled brush, and 3X magnifying mirror. Costs just $7.99 and is available at drug stores and Ulta.

Be careful that there is no underlying makeup or lotion that will make the brow lines look harsher and darker – the products hold onto pigment. Always brush through the brows with a spiral brush after applying any brow product.

For best results, you might want to visit a brow pro at your salon. She will help you shape your brows properly. She can also tint your brows. Even with tinted brows, you might still need to touch up with a pencil or brow powder for a smooth, complete look. Tinting will not fill in missing spots and gaps. Some women regularly schedule their brow appointments along with bikini wax and root touchups.

#4: Use the Rembrandt Technique to Contour Your Face with Makeup

Back in the 1600s, Dutch master painter Rembrandt developed a lighting technique for portraiture that came to be referred to as the triangle of light. In his paintings, Rembrandt concentrated light in an illuminated triangle under the eye of the subject on the less illuminated side of the face. This technique gave depth and texture to Rembrandt's paintings.

Centuries later, pioneering movie director Cecil B. DeMille adopted the technique and was the first to use the term "Rembrandt lighting."

Today, photographers, cameramen, and makeup artists use the triangle of light technique to add contour to the faces of models, movie actresses, and on-air personalities.

You start with foundation which can give you a fresher, healthier looking skin and minimize any sun damage in just minutes. If you have texture problems like lines, flakes, and oversized pores, applying a primer under the foundation can help smooth the way. However, be sure to match the primer to the foundation. If you use a water-based foundation, don't pair it with a silicone-based primer. Use water-based foundations with water-based primers and matching silicone primers with silicone foundations for best results. Be sure to check ingredient lists to be sure.

Apply foundation with your fingers or a foundation brush rather than a sponge for smooth, even coverage. A sponge can deposit too much, making fine lines and large pores more visible. Look for light-diffusing or line-smoothing liquid for a luminous finish. As mentioned earlier, a BB cream works great.

Mineral makeup is good for sensitive skin conditions. It won't clog your pores, so it is ideal if you have problems with breakouts or acne.

If you've been using the same shade of foundation for years, it might be time for a change. Most women choose a shade that is too light. Go at least a half shade to one shade deeper than you think. Choose a warmer shade that is a little on the yellow side for a realistic result. Pink-based foundation gives you a fake "painted lady" look. Avoid foundations with names like cool beige, fair, or rose beige. Instead, look for names that include the words warm, nude, honey, sandy, caramel or golden. A trip to the cosmetic counter at a department store, Sephora or ULTA might be in order to be sure you get the correct color.

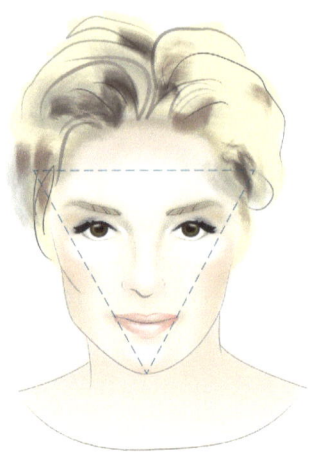

#5: For Best Results, Apply With a High Quality Foundation Brush

You'll want a brush with synthetic bristles. It will make it easier to use less product, manipulate the texture, and blend without leaving streaks or borderlines. Place a small amount of product on the back of your hand, and then use the other hand with a brush to apply in a back and forth motion. Start around the edges of your face and blend inwards. Pat around the edges of the nose, upper checks, and between your nose and upper lip.

If you wear bangs, skip foundation on your forehead because you won't need the coverage and foundation will make your bangs look greasy. Resist applying foundation directly under your eyes – the skin there is thin and prone to crinkling. If you have dark circles which will make your eyes look smaller, use concealer or highlighter to minimize.

Wait until you have applied foundation to your brown spots or dark circles before reaching for concealer. For best results, match your concealer to your foundation which should match your natural skin tone. Use concealer only after foundation and then very sparingly. Apply it with a concealer brush pressed directly over the discoloration. For under-eye dark circles, apply concealer in an upside-down triangle shape below the eye to create an overall brightening effect.

#6: Finish With Powder, Bronzer, Blush

Powder is optional and not for everyone. If you like it, dust on a translucent loose powder or mineral powder using a brush or buff, concentrating on the T-zone.

Add optional bronzer for extra glow. Using a large kabuki brush, swirl it over matte bronzer.

Start at your temple hairline and begin to trace the number 3 on the right side bringing the brush along the edge of your face, back in toward the center of your face directly under your cheekbone towards your mouth, and back out again along the edge of your face under your jawbone ending up at your chin. Repeat a backwards 3 on the left side of your face.

Be sure to blend the bronzer so you can't see the 3's on your face. To make your nose appear thinner, use a smaller brush to apply bronzer down the sides of your nose. You can also apply bronzer to the bottom of your chin and around the upper hairline (not necessary of you wear bangs). Never run bronzer down the center of your nose.

If the bronzer looks to extreme, apply the bronzer first over the foundation – then dust with powder. This is a good daytime look. Apply powder then bronzer for evenings where light will be less intense.

Apply blush high on the cheekbones, starting under your eye pupils. Pink, apricot or berry blushers energize your skin and add realistic warmth. Choose either cream or powder variations. Apply it high up on your cheekbones, not close to the nose or nasolabial folds – the lines that run from the sides of your nose to the sides of your mouth.

With powder blush, use a really big brush. Look straight ahead into the mirror and apply the blush under your pupil and along the cheekbone. Never turn your head – you'll position the color too low on your face. If your blush looks unnatural, switch from cream to powder or vice versa. Powder tends to last longer but cream leaves the most natural-looking flush. However, cream blushes might slide off oily skin while powder can call attention to dry or wrinkled skin.

If you wear bronzer, you still need blush. The brightness of the color of blush wakes up your face and makes the bronzer look more natural.

Apply blush and bronzer with a big, soft brush for even color. Be sure to let your under layers of moisturizer and foundation dry completely before applying blush and bronzer to prevent streaking and blotching.

Note: invest in good brushes and keep them clean. Wash once a week in baby shampoo and let dry overnight.

#7: Lipstick or Lip Gloss?

Lipstick comes in different textures and is great at providing dense, rich color that can last all day. There are 3 main types: Matt to provide a flat color and a long-lasting look; Creamy for those prone to dry lips; and Frosted which are packed with shimmer and are perfect for creating a fuller pout.

Lip gloss comes in all kinds of packages – tubes, pots, and wands. They are perfect for carrying around in your handbag for touch-ups during the day or evening. They do wear off much more quickly than lipstick, so they need to be reapplied often. They come in 4 types: High Shine which gives a wet-looking color; Creamy with the dense color of a lipstick but with a slicker, creamier feel; Sheer and opaque to provide a hint of color and lots of shine; and Sparkling in glitter infused varieties that are perfect for a night out or party.

Layer lip gloss over a lip pencil to achieve more depth of color on thin lips without a heavy lipstick feel. But please, don't wear a dark lip liner – it gives you ring around the mouth and makes you look old and out of date. The best shade of lip liner matches your own real lip color. Also beware of matching your blush to your lip color. Try a cool lip with a warm cheek and vice versa.

For more expert makeup tips, you'll want to refer to *The Makeup Wakeup. Revitalizing Your Look at Any Age* by Lois Joy Johnson (former fashion and beauty editor) and Sandy Linter (celebrity makeup artist).

Chapter 9: Strike Beauty Gold With 13 All Natural Beauty Oils

All skin types and ages can benefit from these amazing natural oils that can be used nightly or applied under moisturizer, foundation, or sunscreen. Many are available at the supermarket – the rest can be obtained at most health food stores or on the Internet at Amazon, Vitacost.com, or other suppliers. Also look for products like beauty creams, shampoos, and conditioners that contain these super additives in their ingredient lists.

#1: **Almond Oil**

Almond Oil is rich in protein, minerals, and vitamins – especially Vitamins E and D – high in oleic, linoleic, and other fatty acids. Great for enhancing hair quality. Also used in the treatment of very dry, chapped skin. Relieves itching, soreness, and inflammation. Use it for removing hard-to-budge eye makeup and mascara. And it's also great for nails and cuticles.

#2: **Argan Oil**

Argan Oil is the new wonder ingredient for hair care products. It can also be used to hydrate skin, strengthen brittle nails, and fight acne. It is rich in essential fatty acids and contains almost twice as much Vitamin E as olive oil making it an excellent skin rejuvenator. Use it for damaged, mature skin and around the eye area. It doesn't clog pores and hydrates all skin types, reduces wrinkles, relieves eczema, dry scalp, psoriasis, and brittle nails. It restores the skin's hydro-lipid layer and prevents the appearance of wrinkles.

#3: Avocado Oil

Avocado Oil is especially helpful for persistently dry skin because of its ability to penetrate the outer layer of your skin. It also has healing properties and helps regenerate cells for both scarred tissue and fine lines. Avocado Oil has high sterol content and contains more Vitamin D than eggs. It is bright green in color due to its Chlorophyll content which quickly turns brown in sunlight, so store in a cool, dark place. It is a superior facial moisturizer due to skin softening and protective properties. It regenerates connective skin tissue while it inhibits bacteria growth. It also stimulates collagen metabolism to slow signs of aging. Therefore, it is often included in anti-aging formulas, because it helps promote cell regeneration and it is especially effective on dry, fragile, distended skin which damages easily.

#4: Coconut Oil

Coconut Oil penetrates the skin very quickly because of its molecular structure. It is rich in both lauric and caprylic acid making it an ideal natural hydrator allowing the skin cells to retain more water to increase strength and elasticity. Makes a gentle exfoliant. Helps with wrinkles, age spots, acne, yeast infections, and sun protection. It strengthens skin's connective tissue and brightens all skin tones.

It is anti-microbial to keep blemishes and acne in check. It also helps with topical yeast and fungal infections. Helps soften rough, dry skin and reduce chronic skin inflammation.

Several recent studies are citing the dementia-reversing effects of eating 1 tsp of raw Coconut Oil each morning. It is also helping sufferers from Parkinson's disease improve cognitive skills. The scientific data is clear – coconut foods can dramatically improve brain chemistry and cognitive function. Coconut Oil helps keep your brain energized by killing unwanted bacteria, balancing hormones, maintaining healthy blood sugar levels, and eliminating brain inflammation.

Choose organic, cold-pressed, food grade Coconut Oil and use it on your skin – plus take a teaspoon or 2 a day orally for mental health.

#5: Emu Oil

Emu Oil won't clog your pores – and it is transdermal – scientifically proven to penetrate the surface layers of the skin. Applying Emu Oil over any antioxidant or peptide-rich product assists the active ingredients in penetrating deep down into the dermis where collagen is stimulated for rejuvenating results. Many plastic surgeons are now advising patients to apply Emu Oil after procedures to heal skin, reduce inflammation and scars and help thicken the skin. It feels oily when you first apply it in the evening, but your skin will feel and look fabulous when your wake up the next morning.

#6: Grapeseed Oil

A light, non-greasy oil available at most grocery stores. It can be used to condition the hair and scalp. Also protects the skin from premature ageing and the accumulation of free radicals. It is a wonderful emollient and a mild astringent to help tighten and tone the skin. It won't clog pores and acts as a nutrient for cell membranes. Rich in Omega 3 and Omega fatty acids to strengthen the lipid barrier in the skin and prevent moisture loss.

#7: Jojoba Oil

Jojoba Oil is used extensively in beauty products like lotions and moisturizers. It is quickly absorbed into the skin and does not leave any oil residue behind. It helps fight wrinkles, stretch marks, and cellulite. Effective on problematic skin conditions like eczema and psoriasis. Soothes irritated skin and increases the natural production of collagen. Provides effective protection against sun and fights the signs of ageing like wrinkles and fine lines.

Can also be used as a hair cleanser and softener. Prevents scalp dryness, soreness, and itchiness. Helps prevent and stop hair loss and thinning hair caused by clogged hair follicles. It dissolves blockages and promotes development of new hair cells which lead to hair growth. Also improves hair texture and appearance – reducing frizzies and dullness. Run a few drops of Jojoba Oil through your hair to make it more manageable.

#8: Marula Oil

Nourishes your skin as it improves moisture balance and elasticity. Easily absorbed – and it won't clog pores. High in oleic acid content, it is perfect for very dry, mature, and ageing skin. Because your skin changes daily, you should change the skin oils you use from time to time. What works one week might not work the next week. Plus your skin benefits from the different nutrients that come from changing up your oils.

To enhance blood flow and relax, simply massage a few drops of Marula Oil into each of the five acupressure facial points: Point 1 is located on the inside edge of eye socket. Point 2 is located at the inside end of each eyebrow. Point 3 is located on the temples behind each eye. Point 4 is located next to each nostril. Point 5 is located under your nose on the midline. Lightly massage under the eyes. You can also massage into cuticles to moisturize and heal damage.

#9: Pomegranate Seed Oil

Pomegranate Seed Oil contains anti-inflammatory properties and high concentrations of anti-oxidants, flavonoids, and fatty acids that nourish and protect dry, mature, and sensitive skin. It helps repair wrinkled, sun-damaged skin – and it's an excellent sunburn remedy because it nourishes and repairs the outer epidermal layer.

#10: Rosehip Seed Oil

Rosehip Seed Oil contains powerful retinoids (Vitamin A), Vitamin E, and essential fatty acids omega 3 and omega 6 making it an ideal topical treatment for resurfacing scarred, hyper-pigmented, or deeply wrinkled skin. Absorbs quickly and cleanly. It has scar reduction properties and is high in linoleic and linoleic acids as well as bioavailable Vitamin C which helps reduce the appearance of dark spots. Rosehip Seed Oil boosts regeneration of the skin and makes it more elastic. It is a natural moisturizer for sensitive, allergic, sun damaged, post-radiation, and burned skin. Excellent treatment for dry skin or scalp, eczema, psoriasis, or uneven skin tones. Be sure to apply sun screen daily when using Rosehip Seed Oil on sun-exposed skin. As a final bonus, regularly dabbing a bit of Rosehip Seed Oil on your nails and cuticles will prevent hangnails and nail breakage.

#11: Shea Butter Oil

Provides protection from the sun and imparts superior softness to the skin with anti-microbial, moisturizing, and hydrating properties. Contains vitamins and allantoin, naturally healing for wrinkles and capillary circulation. Protects against ultraviolet rays that cause sunburn.

#12: Tea Tree Oil

Tea Tree Oil is anti-microbial, anti-septic, anti-viral, anti-bacterial, and anti-fungal. Use for treatment of acne, athlete's foot, herpes, inflamed nail beds, nail fungus, ringworm, dandruff, mites, and scabies. Also effective for treating pimples, oily skin irritation, and rashes. Relieves muscle aches, sprain, and pains. Can be used as an insect repellent, too.

#13: Vitamin E Oil

Vitamin E is a fat soluble vitamin and naturally occurring anti-oxidant. When applied to the skin surface, it is pulled deep into the tissue and absorbed directly into the tissue and cells. Helps protect against changes that lead to skin cancer, wrinkle formation, age spots, and other factors that make your skin appear older than it is.

Chapter 10: Are You a Fashion Victim?

As I am sure you are all well aware, the times have changed and not necessarily for the better. For one thing, the young people have inherited the earth – especially in the worlds of ready-to-wear and retail. I find it harder every year to find clothes that are appropriate for an older woman – by that I mean over 40 – either in size and shape or social context. I don't know about you, but it has taken all the fun out of shopping for me.

Like many of you, I worked in the corporate world in the 80s and 90s requiring a certain level of dressing up and sophistication. Power suits. Elegant dresses. Silk blouses. It was years before the advent of casual Friday which has now morphed into just plain casual...business casual but casual nevertheless.

So, my walk-in closet is filled with clothing that no longer seems appropriate. However, I spent too much money for these things to simply toss them out. So with a full closet, I am often faced with nothing to wear...clothes that don't really fit the way they used to and aren't actually in style.

Additionally, everything else has changed. I am no longer involved in the corporate world. I work at home as a consultant and author – plus I am a licensed Realtor®. I try to work out regularly but my body has changed even though I can still fit into my old outfits. They just don't look the same as they used to.

So what to do? I am not really interested in reinvesting in a lot of new age-appropriate outfits which probably don't actually exist in any event. Here are some things that I am doing to update my look and remain in the game. My goal is to look hip and modern – not like somebody's grandmother even though that I am way old enough to be one.

#1: Edit the Closet

I can't really add too much to my clothing collection without getting rid of some of what I already have. There simply is no more room. Plus my closet recently collapsed under the weight of many decades of investment dressing. Unlike many women, I have not changed in size for many years so I don't have my thin and fat clothes. But if you do, it's time to be honest with yourself and get rid of stuff you haven't been able to fit into for years.

Rule of thumb for everyone: if you haven't worn something for more than a year or 2, it is time for it to go, whether it fits you or not.

Next – condition. If an item is frayed, stained, pilled, too clingy, too short, too saggy or missing buttons, and otherwise in poor repair – OUT! Check your tee shirts and tanks – if they are dingy, gray, and stretched – OUT! Tackle your stack of jeans – can't get the zipper up, too jazzy with designer logos and ornamentation, too low rise or high rise – OUT!

Try on your pants and trousers. If they have high waists, pleated fronts, flared bottoms – OUT. Pants that are out of style are hard to make work, even with the help of a tailor. It is better to toss them and start again.

Here's a tip for summer dressing. If you love white pants and shorts in the summer as I do, don't spend a lot of money on them. Instead, shop for them at the outlet and discount stores, T.J. Maxx, Marshall's, or Costco. Then, when you reach the end of the season and they are dingy, stained and gray – just toss them out. Use the money you save on white bottoms to invest in eye-catching tops.

Check your underwear. Bras that are stretched or cause unsightly bulges – OUT! If you haven't been professionally sized for a bra in the last 10 years, it is time to do so now.

If your bra's band isn't parallel to the floor all around your body, it isn't the right size. You are most likely wearing a band size that is too big – either because you bought the wrong size or the band is stretched out from wear. Try sizing down a width – from 36 to 34 for example. If you get a smaller band size, you probably need to go up one cup size – from a 36C to a 34D. The band should be snug on the loosest hook – so when your bra stretches, you can tighten it.

If you are spilling out over your cups, your bra is too small. Consider a full coverage bra to provide extra support and coverage. If a bigger cup size doesn't resolve your problem, you might need a different style.

However, if you have more room in the cups than you want, switch from a full coverage bra to a demi-cup for great lift with less coverage. You can also try tightening the straps or go down a cup size.

We all hate the dreaded back bulge. If you are having this problem, your band could be too tight or you need a style with a wider back. Look for bras in smooth, stretchy fabrics, or try a longline bra.

Straps that slip can be fixed by tightening the straps. Experts recommend tightening them every other month. If you have narrow or sloped shoulders, a racerback bra might work better for you. Straps that dig might be too tight and need a simple adjustment, or the band is too big and not giving your breasts enough support. Try a smaller band size. Anyone over a D cup should buy a style with narrow straps that are centered on your shoulders so the weight of the breast is evenly distributed.

Now, check your shoes and boots. Are they in good repair – or scuffed and run over at the heels? Those that are – OUT! Stilettos and super-high heels that kill your feet and you can no longer wear for more than 5 minutes – OUT! Colors and styles that are hopelessly outdated – OUT!

Do you have clothing in a lot of odd colors that seemed like a good idea at the time because they were the hot new seasonal color? If so, be honest. Will you really ever find an occasion to wear that lime green jumpsuit again? If not – OUT!

Have you been buying the same things over and over through the years? My personal weakness is chambray shirts. I have a zillion of them. Time to edit my collection – and the rest? OUT! If you have outfits that made you feel great when you bought them but look passé now and rob you of self-confidence when you wear them – OUT!

What to do with the pile of rejects? You can donate them to worthy organizations like the Salvation Army or charities that provide needy women with job-search outfits. You can take your things to a consignment shop which are popping up all over the place. Or you can sell them if they are in good repair on eBay.

What to do with what's left in your closet? Former top fashion and beauty editor and style consultant Lois Joy Johnson recommends that you organize your closet by color to make layering and accessorizing easier. It can cut the time required for dressing in half. Hang all things that are the same color together: jackets, pants, skirts, tops, dresses.

#2: How Do You Make it All Work?

There are several strategies for updating your wardrobe that you should be considering. These are not hard and fast - after all, rules (especially fashion rules) are made to be broken. But at least give these a try.

Aim for a longer neck and longer legs to make you look taller and slimmer. This means V necklines and other low necklines that dip below your collarbone. Nude pumps or flats that match the skin tone of your legs and feet also elongate your look.

Try tonal dressing – one color or shade from head to toe. Again, this will make you look longer and slimmer. The easiest way to do this is with basic black. There isn't a woman in America who doesn't think black makes you look thinner. So a black dress with black tights and black shoes or boots is a no-brainer. But try it with other more vibrant colors, too. Maroon, gray, navy, taupe, camel, cobalt, even red.

Institute a layering policy. This will immediately update your look. It will also help you keep comfortable. If you get too warm, you can always remove a layer or two. But mind the proportions. You want a tall, slim look – that means no baggy tees or chunky knit sweaters. Always try to accent your waist with a handsome belt or jacket that is nipped in at the waist.

Start with the thinnest fabric and the longest layer. That means a long tank or camisole. Add a V-neck, ballet or boat neck tee, then a shirt or blouse followed by a cardigan sweater or jacket. Pair this with a slim bottom –

leggings, skinny jeans or slim ankle cropped pants. Or wear with a pencil skirt.

Again, proportion is key. High volume upper body, slim lower body. High volume lower body – full skirt, wide leg pants – cropped and narrow upper body. If you have a short neck and your bust is large, you should probably avoid the popular infinity scarf. It will make you look bulky and your neck will disappear. If you are short, long cardigans might not work for you – same goes for capri pants. Wear a shorter skirt with opaque tights instead.

Try to create a casual, relaxed look. Master the ½ tuck – tuck the shirt into your bottom in front but leave it out in back. Many of the major designers are showing this look. Wear belts. Narrow ½" to 1" belts work best for most people. But a stunning wider belt can add pizazz to almost any outfit. Roll up the sleeves on your jackets and roll back the cuffs on your shirts. Push up the sleeves of jackets and sweaters for easy nonchalance. Unbutton shirts and blouses at the neckline to create a deep V. If you are wearing a tank underneath, make sure it is showing.

You do not want to be seen in running shoes unless you are headed to the gym. Same goes for yoga pants, sweat pants, and other workout gear. And PLEASE! Save the flannel PJ bottoms for relaxing at home. This look may be ok for a college student – although that is questionable – but it is not ok for you.

Mix prints. Choose small scale prints in 1 color range. It could be a white blouse with small black polka dots combined with a men's wear hound's tooth pant or herringbone skirt. To tie it all together, you can add a solid third piece like a vest in a matching color.

Stick with classics. Classic jeans like Levis or Gap with a mid rise. A classic tan trench coat. The ever-popular classic Little Black Dress – LBD. Classic pencil or A-line skirts that stop at knee level – an inch or 2 above or below is fine – but no minis. Low heels or ballet slippers. Long, slim sweaters in flat knits - ditch the chunky knits that probably make you look fat. Fitted jackets that have stretch and follow the shape of your body – nipped in at the waist. Remove any shoulder pads. Turtlenecks that fit close and have stretch. Fit and flare dresses that look great on everyone – even if you have a pear shape. Stay with classic colors – maroon, gray, black, brown, navy, cobalt, red, camel, taupe. Skip muddy colors, girly pastels, and loud neon brights.

Then take the prim and proper out of classic by layering a tank under your shirt, half tucking the shirt, pushing up or rolling up the sleeves of your jacket or sweater, adding an eye-catching belt to accent your waist or a contrasting colored scarf up near your face.

#3: Let's Talk Shapewear

Hollywood stars with personal trainers, nutritionists, and chefs to keep them slim and svelte often admit to using shapewear for a flawless silhouette on the red carpet, and you should be investing in it, too.

These days, clothing manufacturers seem to have given up completely on linings – even at the higher price points. Shapeware prevents sticking and pulling like linings used to – so clothes won't crease or ride up. Check out shapewear by SPANX that is offered at most major retail outlets. These silky, light compression garments help eliminate unsightly lumps and bumps, and your clothes will fit better. You will probably need bike short shapers in nude and black plus a shaper slip for under dresses. Add new, better-fitting bras and microfiber briefs, and you should be good to go.

#4: Accessories Make the Outfit!

Stylish accessories can turn a blah, out-of-date outfit into something memorable and stunning. Look for statement necklaces and bracelets, colorful scarves, belts, good shoes, and handbags. But don't overdo it. Always remember Coco Chanel's famous words to live by: "when accessorizing, always take off the last thing you put on."

Accessories are investment pieces you can wear over and over in many different ways. You don't have to spend a fortune. I have had a lot of luck finding attractive belts and handbags for not much money at T.J. Maxx and Marshall's. Visit consignment shops and antique malls to find unusual vintage pieces like evening bags, attractive costume jewelry, and Hermes scarves.

Make sure your shoes look up-to-date. You'll need the basics: nude pumps or flats, black heels, neutral flats, and foldable ballet slippers to keep with you always in case your feet start to hurt. Then branch out and add a hair-calf leopard pump plus gold or silver sandals. My personal favorite and signature look is red flats or strappy red heels – these go with almost everything, a new neutral. And they add an unexpected pop to any outfit.

Know when to wear heels and when to wear flats. No one looks stylish hobbling down the street in heels that are too high. Fashionable women stock their closets with shoes that are as comfortable as they are sophisticated. And they know when to sport stilettos and when to rely on a pair of polished flats.

#5: Remember, You Are Not 25 Anymore.

Comfort and age appropriateness should be upmost. Lose the extra-high heels. The accent should be on your shape – not on showing too much flesh. Shirring, ruching, and draping can help disguise body flaws. These designer details keep body contours visible, but they blur the bulges.

Add pizazz to any look with a stylish vest. Down vests in the winter, denim or leather in the other seasons. Look for vests with pockets so you can always have your cell phone handy. Vests hide unsightly back bulges and camouflage muffin top, too.

Another fashion staple: shrugs. Wear them with sleeveless tops and dresses to hide upper arm jiggle and keep you comfortable in air conditioning during the hot summer months. They come in a wide variety of shapes and colors including sweaters that drape or tie at the waist.

#6: Make Sure Your Grooming is Perfect!

You want to look youthful – not silly. Fashionable and polished – not desperate. Classy and successful is the effect you are going for – and that means your grooming must be spot on as well. No roots showing. Whitened teeth for a bright smile. (Brush your teeth with a paste made of baking soda and water a few times a month to whiten your teeth by a shade or 2). Fresh makeup. Beautiful manicure to show off your rings and bracelets. Your outfits should be properly proportioned and look fresh and clean. No spots...no sagging hemlines. And like your mother always told you, standing up straight makes every outfit look better.

#7: Dress for Success and Keep Yourself in the Game!

If you are looking for a job, dress for the job you want, not the one you already have. If you are an independent consultant, you want to project executive polish and competence. Staying current in what you wear keeps you in the game.

When you go for an interview, chances are the interviewer is going to be younger than you are, sometimes a generation or more younger. You probably don't want to look too severely corporate or grown up – and you certainly don't want to remind the interviewer of her mother or grandmother. Don't dust off an old designer power suit from the 90s. Wear a chic dress with or without a jacket. Pay special attention to your shoes, jewelry, and handbag. These are things most human resource people notice.

It is often said that "clothes make the man." They make the woman as well. Put your best foot forward, and create a great new look for yourself. It's easy. It's fun. And it doesn't have to cost a fortune. Plus – when you look great, you feel great – and your self confidence shows.

If this is a topic that interests you, pick up a great book by former fashion and beauty editor Lois Joy Johnson called *The Wardrobe Wakeup. Your Guide to Looking Fabulous at Any Age.* Available on Amazon.

Chapter 11: Gadgets and Gizmos

Getting older is not for sissies. If you want to keep looking your best, it is going to require some extra work and effort – plus some new equipment. Maybe a gym membership and/or personal trainer if you have the money and time – and you are disciplined enough to make it pay.

Here are a few things that I have tried and found to be helpful. Most are available on Amazon so you won't have to search high and low.

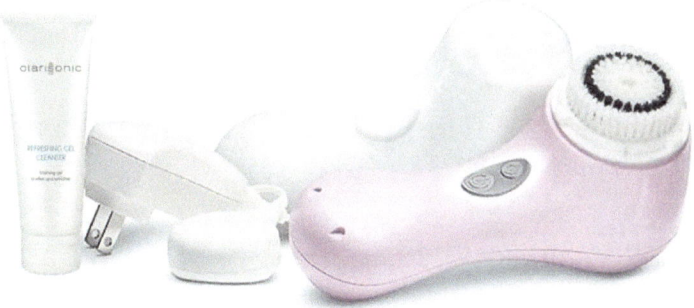

#1: Clarisonic Mia 1 Facial Sonic Cleansing System

This is one of my favorite products ever. And I am not alone. This is a universal big hit with most of the women who have ever tried it.

It cleans your skin 6 times better than using your hands alone. You get a gentle, thorough cleansing for all skin types. Exfoliates so your serums and lotions absorb better after Mia use. Leaves the skin smoother, softer, and more radiant. Gentle enough to use twice daily. Particularly important for removing makeup at night. It is battery operated and waterproof so you can use it in the shower. Comes complete with a Universal pLink battery charger.

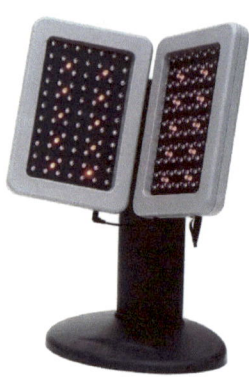

#2: Deep Penetrating Red and Infrared LED Light Therapy

Deep Penetrating Light (DPL) therapy is used for the treatment of pain, relief of muscle and joint aches and sprains, and repairing damaged skin tissues. Use it on your face, neck, hands, arms and body to rejuvenate and plump wrinkles and fine lines, refine pores, fade age spots, reduce inflammation and more. The infrared light stimulates collagen production and affects at least 24 positive changes at the cellular level. It can even help heal diabetic wounds very quickly. It is safe, painless, and scientifically proven effective. NASA, the US Army, and professional athletes have depended on this technology to heal broken bones, torn ligaments, sprains, wounds, and more.

#3: Derma Roller

This is officially called the Micro Needle Roller Skincare Therapy Dermatology System. It consists of a micro-needle roller that works to make you look younger, more vibrant, and with a healthy glow. It helps reduce stretch marks, cellulite, wrinkles, and acne scars. You manually roll it onto areas of the face, neck, thighs, stomach or arms – any place you have skin issues. It stimulates collagen production and texturizes and smooths the look of acne scars and stretch marks. You can use a derma roller to insure deep penetration of topical serums – enhancing their use by as much as 400%. Apply serums like hyaluronic acid, anti-oxidants, and peptides onto clean skin – then use the derma roller.

The derma roller has dozens of tiny needles on a small roller. When you roll it over an area, the needles create little puncture wounds in the upper layer or epidermis of your skin. This triggers the body to create cell turnover and build up collagen in that area.

These rollers are far less costly than chemical peels, and invasive laser treatments with no pain and no downtime. The device comes in needles with three lengths: 0.5mm, 1.0mm and 1.5mm. It is best to start with the shortest, least invasive needles to be sure this is something that you will like and that will work for your skin.

#4: Facial-Flex® Ultra

This amazing product will help you with your facial exercises to improve the muscle tone of your face, chin, and neck with amazing results. Made with surgical steel and space-age materials for years of use. Includes rubber resistance bands in 6 oz. and 8 oz. size. Over time, the Facial-Flex provides an effective, non-surgical facelift particularly in the jowl and jaw line area and in the muscles of the neck and up the side of the face. Use just 2 minutes a day for firmer, stronger facial muscles.

#5: Perfect Fitness Ab Carver Pro

Kinetic engine carbon steel spring turbo-charges your abdominal and arm workouts. Ultra-wide wheel stabilizes movement whether left, right or center. Rubberized non-slip performance grips insure stability and control. Foam kneepad – included – for superior comfort. I particularly like this because you get 2 workouts in 1 – ripped abs and sculpted upper arms. I originally bought this for my husband, but I've taken it over.

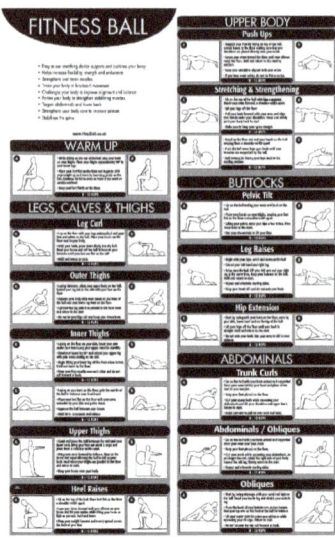

#6: Swiss Stability Ball

These balls come in a variety of sizes that are tailored to your height. They help improve balance, coordination, and flexibility. Ideal for core strength training, stretching, toning, and resistance exercises. Includes 2-way hand pump and comprehensive, illustrated 1-page instruction chart. Order the diameter made for your height: 5'0": 18 inch; 5'1" – 5'6": 22 inch, 5'7" – 6'1": 26 inch, 6'2" – 6'8": 29 ½".

Chapter 12: What If You Get Thrown Out of the Game?

These days, many large companies and corporations are periodically eliminating older employees from their work forces by offering them attractive early retirement packages. They are doing this to cut costs by cutting highly paid senior people and replacing them with more affordable younger workers. There is also a lot of downsizing, outsourcing, and offshoring going on, resulting in more job losses. Add to this job consolidation resulting from mergers and acquisitions and the effects of technological advances and automation – it is no wonder job participation is at a 50-year low.

If you have been swept up by these global forces and you are facing a job loss that you really aren't ready for, what should you do? After all, these are theoretically your peak earning years. The money you should be making could be used to pay down your mortgage or send your kid to college or feather your nest egg.

Plus, if you lose your job, you might need to start drawing down your retirement savings many years before your official retirement age, currently 66. With life expectancy climbing towards 80 or more, spending your retirement savings in your 60s is not a good strategy.

Unfortunately, the same corporate mindset that has decided getting rid of older workers is good strategic thinking also makes it difficult for an older worker to get another job.

Some displaced employees welcome the out because they really weren't happy with their jobs anyway. They managed to climb the ladder at their company through diligence and hard work, but they ended up with a job that was less than satisfying. They always wanted to [fill in the blank]: open a restaurant, become an interior decorator, establish a winery, or become a potter. However, if this isn't you, if you don't have a deep, abiding passion to do something specific, what should you do?

Depending on your background and skills, you could repackage yourself as an independent consultant. This requires a change in the way you look at yourself AND your approach to business. Working for yourself is very different than working as an employee for someone else. It's like flying without a net. There is no guaranteed salary, no health benefits, no paid vacation time, no nothing. It is totally up to you to get yourself some business, fill the pipeline, and start earning money. And once the money starts rolling in, you have to keep accurate records of your expenses and pay your estimated taxes, because there is no automatic withholding either.

First, you must determine if there is a market for your experience. Most consultants find the best target for their services is their former company which still needs the expertise of experienced senior people, even though they have just let a bunch of them go. Other possible targets are the clients or customers of your former company. And don't forget about the competitors of your former company. They are often eager to learn what you know about the company's inner workings, sales philosophies, and strategies.

To be successful as an independent consultant, you'll need a "rent payer" client – a company that puts you on a monthly retainer at a high hourly rate. That way you will be guaranteed a monthly paycheck to cover your expenses, relieving you of a lot of pressure and anxiety. You can then prospect for other smaller clients to provide fill-in work for mad money or retirement savings.

How do you reinvent yourself and adapt to the new career reality? You might need to consult a life or career coach to help you identify where your talents match up to new opportunities to help you create new value.

You probably have much more to offer than you realize. Most of us set up internal prejudices and limiting beliefs that hold us back from optimizing our skills and experience. As a result, many displaced workers need help in reprogramming themselves so they can think of themselves differently and make lemonade out of lemons.

Part of this process is developing a platform which is a unique concept of branding that showcases **your** talents, **your** achievements, and **your** genius. A completed platform includes: your personal brand, your resume and cover letter, supporting materials like a portfolio of past work, letters of recommendations and references, stories of leadership and quantifiable accomplishments, videos, and a Website. Your platform is used to communicate your overall value to an interested hiring manager, recruiter, or company.

The most important element in your platform – and the hardest to complete – is your resume. Your resume needs to create a value message that is communicated to a target employer. It is hard to be objective about yourself and your accomplishments – and it is important to showcase yourself in a way that differentiates you from others competing for the same jobs. Because of this, even skilled resume writers often engage another professional resume writer to help them with their resumes.

There are some widespread misconceptions about resumes and their purpose. First, your resume should be about the future, not the past. For that reason, it is a mistake to start with a summary of accomplishments instead of a fully developed career objective section.

Second, your resume should be about accomplishments, not assignments. You must show how you create value with quantifiable results: sales generated, money saved, efficiencies implemented. And it is about leadership...the assets you can apply to solve problems and address challenges.

Finally, the resume should list only the accomplishments which support your value proposition or career objective. Unrelated experience will only cause the document to lose focus and should be relegated to a short section near the bottom of page 2 or left out altogether.

If this sounds difficult, it's because it is difficult. That's why you will probably need to consult a professional. Can't justify the expense? Consider how much you have invested in your career...college degrees, continuing education, years of on-the-job training, seminars and conferences. Do not be penny wise and pound foolish.

When you are ready to discuss your options with a professional coach, I would suggest you get in touch with one of the best in the country, Donald Burns. Donald has won 10 national awards for his resumes, LinkedIn profiles, cover letters, and bioflyers. He will help you determine your personal brand and build a platform for marketing your unique skills.

This service isn't for everyone. To qualify, you must have 3 perquisites: 1) marketable skills and quantifiable achievements; 2) a professional network of contacts that you have assembled over the years of your career; and 3) the ability and willingness to market your skills and achievements. If this sounds like you, you should get in touch with Donald. He has generously agreed to offer my readers a complimentary 1-hour consultation. It is absolutely free – there is no risk and no obligation. At the end of the hour, you can decide if his services are what you require.

Donald will also be able to determine if you are a good candidate and would benefit from his input. Check out his website at www.ExecutivePromotionsLLC.com. You can reach him at DonaldBurns1@gmail.com. Contact him today to schedule your FREE consultation.

By the way, you don't need to lose your job to be affected by the global employment environment, especially if you are a long-time homemaker. Your husband could lose his job, forcing you to find employment. Or you could be facing another catastrophic loss like a divorce or death of your spouse – both scenarios making it necessary for you get a job to support yourself and your family.

Putting a resume and career plan together after many years of being a stay-at-home mom also requires special skill. I am a certified resume writer specializing in helping people fill the gaps in their work experience. Please contact me at whitneysmith23@verizon.net if you find yourself in this predicament.

Losing your job towards the end of your career does not necessarily mean the end of your income-earning years. You can reinvent yourself and find something worthwhile and fulfilling to do that will also provide you with a living. It is important to keep your spirits up and maintain your enthusiasm while you search for something new to do. Whatever you do, don't withdraw from society and stay in your house. Get out and about. Network with former colleagues. Have lunch or dinner with your friends. Make a determined effort to stay in the game.

SELECTED BIBLIOGRAPHY & RESOURCES

Brownstein, Dr. David, M.D. *Iodine: Why You Need It, Why You Can't Live Without It.* Medical Alternatives Press, 2009.

Denese, Dr. Adrienne, M.D., Ph.D., *Dr. Denese's Secrets for Ageless Skin. Younger Skin in 8 Weeks.* The Berkley Publishing Group, 2005.

Gans, Keri, *The Small Change Diet: 10 Steps to a Thinner, Healthier You.* Gallery Books, 2011.

Goroway, Patricia, *Facial Fitness, Daily Exercises & Massage Techniques for a Healthier, Younger Looking You.* Sterling Publishing Co., Inc., 2010.

Graves, Louisa, *Age-Proof. Beauty Alternatives You Need to Know.* eBookIt.com, 2013.

Graves, Louisa, *Hollywood Beauty Secrets. Remedies to the Rescue.* Bella Publications, 2004.

Isaacs, Greg, *10,000 Steps A Day™ to Optimal Weight. Walk Your Way to Better Health*. Volt Press, 2006.

Johnson, Lois Joy and Linter, Sandy, *The Makeup Wakeup. Revitalizing Your Look at Any Age*. Running Press Book Publishers, 2011.

Johnson, Lois Joy, *The Wardrobe Wakeup. Your Guide to Looking Fabulous at Any Age*. Running Press Book Publishers, 2012.

Lipski, Elizabeth, *Digestion Connection. The Simple, Natural Plan to Combat Diabetes, Heart Disease, Osteoporosis, Arthritis, Acid Reflux – and More!* Rodale Press Inc., 2013.

Perricone, Nicholas, M.D., *Forever Young. Introducing the Metabolic Diet*. Atria Books, division of Simon & Schuster, Inc., 2010.

Wilde, Liz, *Ageless Beauty. The Secrets of Aging Beautifully*. Ryland, Peters & Small, 2006.

Zinczenko, David with Goulding, Matt, *Eat This, Not That, the No-Diet Weight Loss Solution,* Rodale Press Inc., 2014. Note: these books come in annual editions in 3 iterations: the Generic, Supermarket Survival and Restaurant Survival Guides.

www.ingramcontent.com/pod-product-compliance
Lightning Source LLC
Chambersburg PA
CBHW041610220426
43667CB00004B/60